ENCOUNTERING
the
GOODNESS
GOD
of

90 DAILY DEVOTIONS

DESTINY IMAGE BOOKS BY BILL JOHNSON

ENCOUNTERING

the

GOODNESS

GOD

of

90 DAILY DEVOTIONS

• • •

BILL
JOHNSON

DESTINY IMAGE® PUBLISHERS, INC.
P.O. Box 310, Shippensburg, PA 17257-0310
"Promoting Inspired Lives."

This book and all other Destiny Image and Destiny Image Fiction books are available at Christian bookstores and distributors worldwide.

Cover design by Christian Rafetto
Interior design by Terry Clifton

For more information on foreign distributors, call 717-532-3040.
Reach us on the Internet: www.destinyimage.com.

ISBN 13 HC: 978-0-7684-1486-8
ISBN 13 eBook: 978-0-7684-1487-5
ISBN 13 LP: 978-0-7684-1924-5

For Worldwide Distribution, Printed in the U.S.A.
1 2 3 4 5 6 7 8 / 21 20 19 18 17

All devotions adapted from *God is Good*.

OH, TASTE AND SEE THAT
THE LORD IS GOOD...
—PSALM 34:8

WHAT GOD IS LIKE

"GLORY TO GOD IN THE HIGHEST, AND ON
EARTH PEACE, GOODWILL TOWARD MEN!"
—LUKE 2:14

Two thousand years ago, one decree revealed God's heart more clearly than ever before: "Peace and goodwill toward men!" That declaration redefined God's intent for humanity, but after all these years, many of us have not shifted our thinking to be consistent with His announced plan—one of peace and goodwill. Without a shift in thinking, it will be all too easy to misrepresent this magnificent One by expecting and allowing things to take place on our watch that Jesus never would have allowed.

Our boldness to declare and demonstrate who He is in a given situation is seriously impaired if we're not confident of what He is like. When the boldness that is normal within the one filled with the Spirit of God diminishes, it costs us dearly. It is often our boldness that draws Him into an impossible situation. When we know what He is like, we will be able to re-present Jesus as the manifestation of God's goodwill toward men.

● ● ●

PRAYER

Father, I want to know what You are like so I can show people who You are. Teach my heart how to see You more clearly.

THE ANSWER IS JESUS

"THE THIEF COMES ONLY TO STEAL AND KILL AND DESTROY; I CAME THAT THEY MAY HAVE LIFE, AND HAVE IT ABUNDANTLY. I AM THE GOOD SHEPHERD; THE GOOD SHEPHERD LAYS DOWN HIS LIFE FOR THE SHEEP."
—JOHN 10:10-11

Many Christians think God causes or allows evil to take place so He can display His mercy, but that would be like me breaking my child's arm to show my ability to give him comfort, and then using my skills to reset the broken bone. People ask me, "What about Job?" My response is, "What about Jesus?"

Job provides the question. Jesus gives the answer. The story of Job is about holding to our faith in the midst of trials and seeing God restore everything brilliantly, but the story of Jesus is the only one I follow. There's no question that God can turn any situation around for His glory and for our benefit—this, of course, includes the most evil conditions known to humanity around the world. But that is the testimony of His greatness and His redemptive purpose. It does not represent His design.

Jesus gave us all we needed to know. "I came that they may have life, and have it abundantly" (John 10:10-11). It's not complicated. Loss, death, and destruction are the things left behind when the devil has had influence in a given situation. Jesus is the Good Shepherd. What does that goodness look like? He gives abundant life.

• • •

PRAYER

Lord, I want to be able to see You even in the midst of pain. You are my answer in the swirl of life's questions.

GOD AND DISCIPLINE

THE SON OF GOD APPEARED FOR THIS PURPOSE,
TO DESTROY THE WORKS OF THE DEVIL.
—1 JOHN 3:8

If I were to do to my children what many people think
God does to His children, I'd be arrested for child
abuse. People say God is good, yet they credit Him with
causing cancer and natural disasters and even blame Him
for terrorist activities. They constantly embrace a hellish
situation in their lives because of the thought that God
intended it for good.

That way of thinking infects the God-given ability
to discern the works of the devil with a human reasoning
that is demonic in nature. In fact, it's not just discernment
that is in question—this kind of breakdown in our assignment to spiritual maturity causes us to forget who the
enemy really is and what we're actually fighting against.

Jesus taught us how to recognize the works of the
devil and then modeled how we destroy them. Do we have

the right to set a new way of life and ministry that doesn't do what Jesus commanded us to do? Absolutely not!

It is time to reexamine our belief system and find out what the Bible really teaches about the nature of God.

● ● ●

PRAYER

Lord, help me to see You as You are. I want to know You as my good Father, who gives good gifts to His kids.

WE CAN'T EXAGGERATE HIS GOODNESS

OH, TASTE AND SEE THAT THE LORD IS GOOD;
BLESSED IS THE MAN WHO TRUSTS IN HIM!
—PSALM 34:8

Either He is authentically good, or He is not. I would never suggest that we pretend He is different than He is. Nothing is accomplished by allowing our imagination to create our own image of God. He would then be no better than the gods made out of wood or stone, also created by human initiative. Inventing Him in our minds or building Him with our hands is a similarity that is both vain and ultimately destructive.

Discovering who He is and what He is like in reality is the only possible way to discover His true goodness. This eternal journey into His infinite goodness is the one we are privileged to embrace.

It's impossible for us to create a concept of what He is like that is greater than He really is. He is either greater than we can understand, perceive, describe, or imagine, or He is not God—we are.

Neither can we exaggerate His goodness. We can twist it, pervert it, dilute it, and misrepresent it. But the one thing we cannot do is exaggerate the goodness of God. It will take us all of eternity just to broach the subject of His goodness.

PRAYER

Father, open my heart to behold Your goodness. I am a witness of Your goodness on the earth.

WE NEED TO EXPERIENCE HIS GOODNESS

TRUST IN THE LORD WITH ALL YOUR HEART,
AND LEAN NOT ON YOUR OWN UNDERSTANDING.
—PROVERBS 3:5

Things are about to change. The greatest harvest of souls of all time is about to come in, and it won't come because of our advanced skills in preaching, our use of media, or even our powerful music. Each of those areas has importance, but they do not exist unto themselves. They are important in that they are vehicles that carry the greatest revelation of all time—God is good, and He is a perfect Father.

His goodness is beyond our ability to comprehend, but not our ability to experience. Our hearts will take us where our heads can't fit. Understanding is vital, but it often comes through experiencing God. Faith for the journey of walking with God leads to encounters with God. It results in a growing knowledge and understanding of truth, as in " by faith we understand that the worlds were framed by the word of God" (Heb. 11:3).

Having said that, one of the great commands of Scripture pertaining to the experience of His goodness is "taste and see that the Lord is good" (Ps. 34:8). If you'll taste it for yourself, you'll see it more clearly. Your perception of truth will increase as you experience truth more deeply.

● ● ●

PRAYER

Lord, thank You that I don't have to understand before I put my trust in You. You are good all the time.

THE REALITY OF WHO HE IS

BE STILL, AND KNOW THAT I AM GOD.
—PSALM 46:10

I've heard people say they don't believe in God anymore after experiencing a disappointment or tragic loss of some sort. I don't mean to treat their situation with disregard, but you can't turn a consciousness of God on and off like that. You may be mad at God. You may accuse Him and refuse to serve Him, but you can't decide He no longer exists.

To claim atheism as a belief system doesn't get rid of Him. It merely deadens a person's awareness of Him and attempts to remove the awareness of his need for Him from the context of daily life. Merely changing our theology changes us, not Him.

But when what we believe is anchored in the reality of who He is, earth comes into agreement with Heaven where the reality of His world increasingly invades ours, manifested in both power and glory.

His goodness is beyond our ability to comprehend, but not our ability to experience. Our hearts will take us where our heads can't fit.

● ● ●

PRAYER

Lord, I want Your truth to come and be a part of me, until even my thoughts begin to look like You. Help me to renew my mind, so I can be filled up with your truth.

BEYOND ALL WE ASK OR THINK

NOW TO HIM WHO IS ABLE TO DO FAR MORE ABUNDANTLY BEYOND ALL THAT WE ASK OR THINK, ACCORDING TO THE POWER THAT WORKS WITHIN US, TO HIM BE THE GLORY IN THE CHURCH AND IN CHRIST JESUS TO ALL GENERATIONS FOREVER AND EVER. AMEN.

—EPHESIANS 3:20-21

The phrase "beyond all that we ask or think" is quite impressive. "Beyond all we ask" addresses the impact of our prayers, which include both those that are outwardly expressed as well as the secret cries of the heart. What God does for us is beyond the reach of our biggest prayer on our greatest day with our highest level of faith—He exists in that realm to work for us.

"Beyond all we think" is another very powerful statement dealing with the impact of our imagination. This describes us on our best day, with our most well-thought-out dreams, plans, goals, and imaginations. His commitment to us is to function beyond the limitations of our imagination and perform the unthinkable on our behalf. These are expressions of His goodness, which come from His being. He is perfect goodness personified.

I said "yes" to this journey many years ago and have since discovered that His goodness is beyond my wildest dreams.

• • •

PRAYER

Father, I say "yes" to Your goodness. I want to see it in my everyday life, even in areas where I don't expect it to be.

DAY 8

THE TRUE DISCOVERY
OF HIS GOODNESS

THOUGH I SPEAK WITH THE TONGUES
OF MEN AND OF ANGELS, BUT HAVE
NOT LOVE, I HAVE BECOME SOUNDING
BRASS OR A CLANGING CYMBAL.
—1 CORINTHIANS 13:1

The one thing that concerns me most in the day in which we live is the possibility of another civil war. It isn't racial, political, or economic. Neither is it fought between groups with differing moral or social agendas. While those tensions obviously exist in society, they have permission to exist because of the division that is celebrated in the Church. We set the stage. It's tough to get reconciliation in the factions that exist in the world around us when the Church itself sponsors the wars of internal conflict with religious delight.

I'm referring to a war within the family of God—it is spiritual. It's being fought with words of accusation, character assassination, ridicule, and slander. The conflict is over the goodness of God. That spirit of accusation is welcomed in many circles as the voice of reason, the voice of discernment.

The Church isn't known for handling conflict well. We tend to be the only army in the world that shoots their wounded, especially if they were wounded through their own doing. Good theology is essential. But theology without love is a loud clanging cymbal—annoying at best. I believe that a true discovery of the goodness of God could heal this issue for us all.

● ● ●

PRAYER

Lord, I need to know Your goodness! Help me to keep my eyes on You and learn to think with love.

DAY 9

RENEWING YOUR MIND

AND DO NOT BE CONFORMED TO THIS WORLD,
BUT BE TRANSFORMED BY THE RENEWING
OF YOUR MIND, SO THAT YOU MAY PROVE
WHAT THE WILL OF GOD IS, THAT WHICH
IS GOOD AND ACCEPTABLE AND PERFECT.
—ROMANS 12:2

A renewed mind is made available to us as a gift from a good Father—it is the mind of Christ. The renewed mind is more than having the ability to give a biblical answer to a problem. It includes that, but in reality it is so much more. It is seeing from a divine perspective.

In Romans 12:2 the renewed mind proves the will of God. That is fascinating when you realize that the best definition for the will of God in Scripture is Matthew 6:10: "Your will be done, on earth as it is in heaven." It can be said that the renewed mind is what reveals and illustrates God's will on earth. The mind of Christ, seen in Jesus' lifestyle, demonstrates this beautifully. He confronted storms, healed bodies, multiplied food, and did countless other miracles to reveal Heaven's effect on earth. The renewed mind in us should do the same.

We will know our mind is renewed when the impossible looks logical.

● ● ●

PRAYER

Father, help me to think the way You think and see from Your perspective. I know that You are good, and I want Your goodness to be my platform for life.

DEALING WITH FALSE WORDS

"BLESSED ARE THE MERCIFUL, FOR
THEY SHALL RECEIVE MERCY."
—MATTHEW 5:7

If someone calls me on the phone and tells me that the sickness I am suffering from has been given to me by God to teach me to trust Him, I need to examine his word to see if it is an authentic word from God. Tragically, many "forgeries" are accepted by believers day after day and then sold to others in the Christian marketplace as authentic revelations of the will of God.

There's not one example of Jesus giving a disease to anyone. In fact, His lifestyle was the opposite. What the person claims is an authentic word from God contradicts the examples of His known works. The renewed mind is able to come to the conclusion that what was given to me with God's signature at the bottom is in fact a forgery. The nature of this deceptive piece is so severe that it requires me to expose it as a fraud so that no one buys the counterfeit art in His name.

Even though I soundly reject this person's word to me, I don't reject the person. I know that my approach to that person sets the standard for how I am to be treated in my day of need.

●　●　●

PRAYER

Father, help me to remember to walk in love, especially when I know that someone else is wrong. I want to love the way You do.

USING THE ORIGINAL STANDARD

"MOST ASSUREDLY, I SAY TO YOU, HE WHO
BELIEVES IN ME, THE WORKS THAT I DO HE WILL
DO ALSO; AND GREATER WORKS THAN THESE
HE WILL DO, BECAUSE I GO TO MY FATHER."
—JOHN 14:12

Mostly every believer confesses that God is good. We have to—it's in the Bible. It's not the belief in His goodness that threatens us. It's our definition of this goodness that has brought much debate and sometimes conflict and turmoil into the family of God.

If He is as good as many claim, how we respond to this truth will require massive change in how we do life. Creating doctrines of no miracles today not only contradicts His Word, it is a sneaky way to avoid responsibility.

For two thousand years, we've been comparing ourselves to the previous generation, noticing only slight differences. And to console ourselves with the task at hand—the Great Commission to disciple nations, displaying the greater works of Jesus—many create watered-down doctrines that dismantle the example and commandments Jesus gave us.

Instead of comparing ourselves with ourselves, we should have been using the original standard found in the life of Jesus so that the measure of God's goodness revealed in Christ would have remained the same through the past two thousand years. God is bringing us back to the original measurement so that He might be revealed more accurately as the Father who loves well.

● ● ●

PRAYER

Lord, would You help me to live as Jesus lived while on the earth? I want to share Your love with the people around me.

GOD DOESN'T DO
BAD THINGS

GREAT MULTITUDES FOLLOWED HIM,
AND HE HEALED THEM ALL.

—MATTHEW 12:15

Nowhere in the Gospels do we see Jesus giving someone a sickness. Some say, "He allowed it," instead of, "He caused it," but in my way of thinking, there's little to no difference. If I abuse my children, or "allow/approve" a neighbor to do it, it's obvious I have a very serious problem.

To attribute evil to God tragically undermines our purpose on the earth. Namely, it cripples our ability to represent Jesus as the manifestation of God's goodness. It really comes down to this—many have rejected the clear revelation of the nature of God that is seen in the person of Jesus Christ.

The view of God causing evil ultimately compromises our ability to discern the difference between God's discipline and an actual demonic assault. And that is a weakness we cannot afford to carry around any longer.

Loss, death, and destruction.

Abundant life.

One is bad; the other is good. It shouldn't be that hard to distinguish between the two. Instead of creating doctrines that explain away our weakness and anemic faith, we need to find out why "the greater works than these" have not been happening in and around us (see John 14:12).

● ● ●

PRAYER

Father, help me to look at Jesus' life in the Gospels and see You as You are. I want to know You through His life.

TRUTH, NOT LIES

"IF YOU HAD KNOWN ME, YOU WOULD HAVE
KNOWN MY FATHER ALSO; AND FROM NOW
ON YOU KNOW HIM AND HAVE SEEN HIM."
—JOHN 14:7

A person is to be valued for who he is in God, not because he gets everything right. None of us do. In the Old Testament, the prophet was judged if he gave a wrong word. In the New Testament, the word is to be judged.

Many good people believe lies, and they must be treated with kindness—they were poisoned with a lie. But it's equally true that the lies they promote must be exposed as forgeries. The biggest forgery of all just might be the teaching that Jesus no longer heals people from sickness and delivers them from torment. Simple examination of Scripture proves that such a concept is a devilish misrepresentation of the One who gave Himself to reveal the Father and redeem humanity.

What causes me the most grief is that this way of thinking misrepresents the nature of God. It hurts our approach to life, seriously damaging our ability to represent Him as good. Perhaps it's these forgeries that have been marketed for decades by well-meaning believers that have contributed to the single greatest vacuum in human consciousness—the knowledge of the goodness of God.

●　●　●

PRAYER

Lord, I want to have a true image of You. If I believe any lies about You and Your goodness, would You show me Your truth?

THE TRANSFORMING POWER OF GOD

"YOU WILL KNOW THE TRUTH, AND THE
TRUTH WILL MAKE YOU FREE."
—JOHN 8:32

God longs to reveal Himself to those who are ready to fully embrace what they discover. In many ways our yes precedes seeing more of Him. Our yes is our invitation for more of Him.

Revelation of truth releases responsibility for truth. Revelation is seldom given to those who are merely curious. You'll never see Him reveal truth just to make us smarter or more capable of debating with those who see differently. Truth by nature is the transforming power of God to instill freedom in the life of those who embrace it.

My journey starts to break down when my thoughts violate who He is. When our questions express our hunger for discovery, they're fruitful. But when our questions challenge who He is, they are foolish and lead to intellectual pride and ultimately spiritual barrenness.

It could be said that freedom exists in a person's life to the degree he embraces truth from the heart. It's more than a mental agreement to a concept called truth. It is the heartfelt yes to a way of life. That way of life becomes measurable in our lifestyle of freedom.

● ● ●

PRAYER

Father, You have filled my life with joy. I get to walk in Your presence and know the greatest kind of joy.

SUBDUE THE EARTH

"BE FRUITFUL AND MULTIPLY; FILL
THE EARTH AND SUBDUE IT."
—GENESIS 1:28

Man was created in the image of God and placed into the Father's ultimate expression of beauty and peace—the Garden of Eden. Outside of that garden, it was a different story. It was without the order and blessing contained within and was in great need of the touch of God's delegated one—Adam.

It's an amazing thought to consider that something could be so perfect and good from God's perspective, yet be incomplete. God Himself longed to see what those who worshiped by choice would do with what He gave them to steward.

God's command to subdue the earth reveals something that is often ignored. The Garden of Eden was perfect, but the rest of the planet was in disarray. Outside of the Garden was chaos and disorder as it was under the influence of the devil and his hordes. For that reason, a military term was used to describe Adam and Eve's assignment. In a sense they were born into a war. They were to bring the earth under their control and ultimately under the influence of God through their righteous rule.

Discovering God's original commission and purpose for mankind can help to fortify our resolve to a life of history-shaping significance.

● ● ●

PRAYER

Lord, I want to work with You to carry out Your purposes on the earth. Would you show me what "subduing the earth" looks like for me and my family?

BE FRUITFUL AND MULTIPLY

"BUT OTHERS FELL ON GOOD GROUND AND
YIELDED A CROP: SOME A HUNDREDFOLD,
SOME SIXTY, SOME THIRTY."
—MATTHEW 13:8

The backbone of Kingdom authority and power is found in our commission, and the first commission given to mankind was "Be fruitful." This is a specific command to be productive. It included discovering the laws of God's creation and cooperating with them to make the ever-expanding Garden a better place. God was not afraid of Adam and Eve personalizing His creation. Their mark of delegated authority was to be seen in their management of creation itself.

They were to have children, who in turn would have children, and so on. It was God's intention that as they bore more children, who also lived under God's rule, they would be able to extend the boundaries of His Garden through the simplicity of their devotion to Him. Because they were His delegated authority, they could display the beauty of God's Kingdom by representing Him well.

The greater the number of people in right relationship to God, the greater the impact of their leadership. This process was to continue until the entire earth was covered with the glorious rule of God through man.

● ● ●

PRAYER

Father, Your testimonies in my life are good. I am so thankful that I get to see You as You work.

FILL THE EARTH

NOW THANKS BE TO GOD WHO ALWAYS
LEADS US IN TRIUMPH IN CHRIST, AND
THROUGH US DIFFUSES THE FRAGRANCE
OF HIS KNOWLEDGE IN EVERY PLACE.

—2 CORINTHIANS 2:14

Because satan had rebelled and had been cast out of Heaven with a portion of the fallen angels and had taken dominion of the earth, it becomes obvious why the rest of the planet needed to be subdued—it was under the influence of the powers of darkness (see Gen. 1:2). God could have destroyed the devil and his host with a word; instead, He chose to defeat darkness through His delegated authority—those made in His image who were lovers of God by choice.

"Fill the earth" (Genesis 1:28). God's target was the entire planet. One can only imagine what that might have looked like had Adam and Eve not sinned—humanity living in perfect harmony, under One God, all working to glorify God through their management of what He had

created. Every corner of the earth was to feel the influence of His delegated ones, who served and ruled out of love—love for God, love for one another, and love for all that He had made.

● ● ●

PRAYER

The sound of Your voice gives me hope. I am so thankful that I get to hear it.

UNDER THE AUTHORITY OF GOD ALMIGHTY

"LORD, I AM NOT WORTHY FOR YOU TO COME UNDER MY ROOF, BUT JUST SAY THE WORD, AND MY SERVANT WILL BE HEALED. "FOR I ALSO AM A MAN UNDER AUTHORITY, WITH SOLDIERS UNDER ME."
—MATTHEW 8:8-9

The Sovereign One placed us—Adam's children—in charge of planet Earth, even though we were only capable of managing a small portion to start with. He did something similar with the children of Israel when He gave them all of the Promised Land. He basically told them, "It's all yours, although I'll give it to you little by little." He then went on to explain that the timing of the release of their inheritance was for their sake, so the beasts of the field wouldn't become too numerous for them. This is remarkable. From day one, God has longed for His people to rule out of their right relationship with Him.

The centurion brilliantly illustrates this same principle when He asks Jesus to heal his servant in Matthew 8:7-10. Because the centurion was under authority, he knew he had authority. Adam and Eve were given a huge assignment, which depended on their relationship with God, not their gifts and talents alone. Their authority was based entirely on being under the authority of the Almighty God.

● ● ●

PRAYER

Father, help me understand that I am operating out of Your authority. I want to think Your thoughts and do what You are doing.

DOMINION EMPOWERS

Satan didn't come into the Garden of Eden and violently take possession of Adam and Eve. He couldn't—He had no dominion there. Dominion empowers. And because man was given the keys of dominion over the planet, the devil would have to get his authority from man. The suggestion to eat the forbidden fruit was simply the devil's effort to get Adam and Eve to agree with him in opposition to God, thus empowering him. To this day it is through agreement that the devil is able to kill, steal, and destroy. He is still empowered through man's agreement.

Mankind's authority to rule was forfeited when Adam ate the forbidden fruit. In that one act, mankind went from ruler over a planet to the slave and possession of the evil one. All that Adam owned, including the title deed to the planet with its corresponding position of rule, became part of the devil's spoil.

But God's predetermined plan of redemption immediately kicked into play. Jesus would come to reclaim all that was lost.

● ● ●

PRAYER

Father, You have done wonderful works in my life! You have saved me out of darkness and brought me into Your light.

KEYS OF AUTHORITY

"FOR THE SON OF MAN HAS COME TO SEEK
AND TO SAVE THAT WHICH WAS LOST."
—LUKE 19:10

God's plan of rulership for man never ceased. Jesus came to bear man's penalty for sin and recapture what had been lost. Not only was mankind lost to sin, his dominion over planet Earth was also lost. Jesus came to recapture all that was lost.

The devil was kicked out of Heaven because he considered himself equal to God and deserving of worship. And while he knew he wasn't worthy of Jesus' worship, he also knew that Jesus had come to reclaim the authority man had given away. Satan had those keys of authority that man lost through sin. He told Jesus, *"All this authority I will give You, and their glory; for this has been delivered to me"* (Luke 4:6).

Notice the phrase "for this has been delivered to me." Satan could not steal it. It had been relinquished when

Adam abandoned God's rule. It was as though satan was saying to Jesus, "I know what You came for. You know what I want. Worship me, and I'll give the keys back." In effect he offered Jesus a shortcut to His goal of recapturing those keys. But Jesus said "no" to the shortcut and refused to give him any honor. There were no shortcuts to His victory.

● ● ●

PRAYER

Father, I will praise You for as long as I live. Your works are wonderful, and I have seen them.

THINKING HIS THOUGHTS

FOR AS HE THINKS IN HIS HEART, SO IS HE.
—PROVERBS 23:7

Entertaining a lie is a poison that works into our being to destroy our identity and purpose. The devil lies about who God is and, in turn, who we are. It's all about identity. Through rebellion, satan lost his place of identity with God for eternity. He is trying to do the same to the only part of all creation that was made in God's image.

I can't afford to have a thought in my head about me that He doesn't have in His head about me. Thinking independently of God is not freedom. In fact, it is the worst possible bondage imaginable to think outside of the purpose and design set in place by the greatest creative genius ever to exist. The mind-boggling challenge comes when we realize that this One who owes us nothing has invited us into a co-laboring role in caring for all He has made through the privileged relationship of discovering His heart. As a result, the greatest gift we can give ourselves is to require that our thought life work in tandem with His goodness. Being tethered to His goodness is the most wonderful illustration of freedom and liberty possible.

● ● ●

PRAYER

Lord, I have seen Your beauty in my life. My life is a testimony of Your greatness.

THE ORIGINAL PLAN

LET THE REDEEMED OF THE LORD
SAY SO, WHOM HE HAS REDEEMED
FROM THE HAND OF THE ENEMY.

—PSALM 107:2

Satan was defeated by a man—the Son of Man—who was rightly related to God. Now, as people receive the work of Christ on the cross for salvation, they become grafted into that victory. Jesus defeated the devil with His sinless life, defeated him in His death by paying for our sins with His blood, and defeated him again in the resurrection, rising triumphant with the keys of authority over all, including death, hell, and the grave.

In redeeming man, Jesus recovered what man had given away. From the throne of triumph He declared, *"All authority has been given to Me in heaven and on earth. Go therefore"* (Matt. 28:18). In other words: "I got the keys back. Now go use them and reclaim what was lost."

God's original plan was never aborted; it was fully realized once and for all in the resurrection and ascension of Jesus. We were then to be completely restored to His plan of ruling as a people made in His image. As such, we would learn how to enforce the victory obtained at Calvary: "The God of peace will soon crush Satan under your feet" (Rom. 16:20).

● ● ●

PRAYER

Lord, You have made my life victorious. I walk in victory, because of You and what You have done through Your Son.

BORN TO RULE

"HEAL THE SICK, CLEANSE THE LEPERS,
RAISE THE DEAD, CAST OUT DEMONS. FREELY
YOU HAVE RECEIVED, FREELY GIVE."
—MATTHEW 10:8

We were born to rule—rule over creation, over darkness—to plunder hell, to rescue those headed there, and to establish the rule of Jesus wherever we go by preaching the Gospel of the Kingdom. Kingdom means King's domain, King's dominion. In the original purpose of God, mankind ruled over creation. Now that sin has entered the world, creation has been infected by darkness, such as disease, sickness, afflicting spirits, poverty, natural disasters, and demonic influence. Our rule is still over creation, but now it is focused on exposing and undoing the works of the devil. We are to give what we have received to reach that end.

If I truly receive power from an encounter with the God of power, I am equipped to give it away. The invasion of God into impossible situations comes through a people who have received power from on high and have learned to release it into the circumstances of life.

● ● ●

PRAYER

Lord, You are great in my life and You have done great things. I am so pleased that I get to walk this earth with You.

LIVING BY FAITH

FOR WHATEVER IS NOT FROM FAITH IS SIN.
—ROMANS 14:23

One of the tragedies of a weakened identity is how it affects our approach to Scripture. Many, if not most, theologians make the mistake of taking all the good stuff contained in the prophets and sweeping it under that mysterious rug called the Millennium. It is not my desire to debate that subject right now. But I do want to challenge our thinking and deal with our propensity to put off those things that require courage, faith, and action to another period of time. The mistaken idea is this: if it is good, it can't be for now.

A cornerstone in this theology is that the condition of the Church will always be getting worse and worse; therefore, tragedy in the Church is just another sign of these being the last days. In a perverted sense, the weakness of the Church confirms to many that they are on the right course. I have many problems with that kind of thinking, but only one I'll mention now—it requires no faith!

It's time for a revolution in our vision. Vision starts with identity and purpose. Through a revolution in our identity, we can think with divine purpose, and such a change begins with a revelation of Him.

● ● ●

PRAYER

Lord, You are truth. My heart longs to know Your goodness more deeply.

YOU HAVE WORTH IN HIS SIGHT

TO HIM WHO IS ABLE TO DO EXCEEDINGLY
ABUNDANTLY ABOVE ALL THAT WE
ASK OR THINK, ACCORDING TO THE
POWER THAT WORKS IN US.

—EPHESIANS 3:20

Embracing a belief system that requires no faith is dangerous and is in itself a contradiction in terms. It is contrary to the nature of God and all that the Scriptures declare. He plans to do "above all we could ask or think," according to Ephesians 3:20, so His promises by nature challenge our intellect and expectations. "[Jerusalem] *did not consider her destiny; therefore her collapse was awesome*" (Lam. 1:9). The result of forgetting our destiny and His promises is not one we can afford.

We are often more convinced of our unworthiness than we are of His worth. Our inability takes on greater focus than does His ability. But the same One who called fearful Gideon a "valiant warrior" and unstable Peter a "rock" has called us the Body of His beloved Son on earth. That has to count for something. The very fact that He declares it makes the impossible possible.

Those who walk in arrogance because of how they see themselves in Christ don't really see it at all. When we see who He is, what He has done on our behalf, and who He says we are, there is only one possible response—worship from a humble and surrendered heart.

● ● ●

PRAYER

Father, You have done great things for me. Everything You do is lovely and good.

WORTH THE RISK

"THEN I WILL GIVE THEM A HEART TO
KNOW ME, THAT I AM THE LORD; AND
THEY SHALL BE MY PEOPLE, AND I WILL
BE THEIR GOD, FOR THEY SHALL RETURN
TO ME WITH THEIR WHOLE HEART."
—JEREMIAH 24:7

God didn't create us to be robots. He made us to be powerful expressions of Himself. When He did this, He made it possible for Him to feel heartache and pain from our choices. All parents understand this pain. He took a risk by giving us a choice to serve Him, ignore Him, or even mock Him. The Perfect One chose vulnerability, a willingness to be influenced by what He has made, over the squeaky clean world that the robots could manage without disrupting His plan.

Why did He consider it worth the risk? What was He looking for?

People, those made in His image, who took their place before Him as worshipers, as sons and daughters, as those whose very natures are immersed in His. They would become co-laborers in managing, creating, and contributing to the well-being of all He has made. From His perspective it was worth the risk.

● ● ●

PRAYER

Lord, my heart is at home in Your presence. I get to taste and see Your goodness in my life and the lives of my family.

LIBERTY IN THE SPIRIT

STAND FAST THEREFORE IN THE LIBERTY
BY WHICH CHRIST HAS MADE US FREE.
— GALATIANS 5:1

Our freedom of choice is so valuable to Him that He restrains Himself from manifesting His presence in a way where our freedom of choice would be removed. That may sound strange to some, but when He reveals Himself in fullness, even the devil and his demons will declare that Jesus Christ is Lord.

Some realities are so overwhelming, like the full manifestation of God's glory, that there's little room for reason and choice. God has chosen to veil Himself in just the right measure so that our wills and intellects could be shaped by our allegiance to Him. He is there for anyone humble enough to recognize his or her personal need. He is also subtle enough to be ignored by those who are filled with themselves.

Liberty, then, is not doing as we please. It's having the ability to do what is right. Real freedom is given to the humble because pride restricts, restrains, and leads to smallness. Liberty is the result of being freed by the Holy Spirit Himself, who demonstrates the fruits and benefits of coming under the Lordship of Jesus Christ. There's more room in the Kingdom of God than outside it.

● ● ●

PRAYER

Your cry of freedom pulses in my heart. You have set me free.

CREATION AND THE CREATOR

THE FEAR OF THE LORD IS THE
BEGINNING OF WISDOM.
—PSALM 111:10; PROVERBS 9:10

The enemy of our souls wars against everything that leads to true freedom. One of the great tragedies of this present day is that for the most part, our educational systems have succeeded in removing the concept of a creator from people's way of thinking and daily lifestyle. In doing so, society abandons its moral compass and loses the awareness of a code to live by. The moral compass is then replaced by what is popular in the moment, which constantly changes according to whoever has the microphone. Political correctness is the outcome. And it is here we find the evidence that stupidity is contagious. Insanity becomes flaunted as sanity, and the absence of moral responsibilities then becomes the doctrine of the day.

Consider this: When there is no creator, there is no design. When the concept of design is removed from our thinking and our lifestyles, then we lose the sense of purpose. When purpose is out of the equation, so also is the idea of an eternal destiny. And by removing eternity from the thoughts of a people, we also lose the sense of accountability. And when accountability is gone, so is the fear of the Lord.

● ● ●

PRAYER

Father, I want to live my life in such a way that I bring hope to those around me. May people be able to look at me and see You.

THE FEAR OF THE LORD

Oh, taste and see that the Lord is good;
blessed is the man who trusts in Him!
—PSALM 34:8

The fear of the Lord is significantly different than many interpret. It's not a fear that drives us from God, but one that draws us to Him. It is endearing in nature, and it is as essential for New Testament believers as it was in the Old Testament. This is wisdom. Wisdom is the essential building block for us to be able to fulfill our reason for being. Understanding how God created us and the purpose for our creation goes a long way in our correctly interpreting life on this planet without mistakenly questioning the goodness of God whenever we see a problem.

For some this may seem like a giant too big to kill—an insurmountable task. Not so. All isms, whether it's socialism, communism, Hinduism, Buddhism, or the like, cower in the face of an authentic Gospel, one of purity and power. Live it as Jesus lived it, say it as Jesus said it, and display it as Jesus displayed it. People will abandon everything inferior if they can but taste and see from the authentic Gospel of the Kingdom.

• • •

PRAYER

Lord, teach me Your ways, so I can walk in your truth. May Your light shine in my life.

RESCUED FROM A LIE

HE HAS DELIVERED US FROM THE POWER
OF DARKNESS AND CONVEYED US INTO
THE KINGDOM OF THE SON OF HIS LOVE,
IN WHOM WE HAVE REDEMPTION THROUGH
HIS BLOOD, THE FORGIVENESS OF SINS.
—COLOSSIANS 1:13-14

Lies are costly, as they steal life from all who embrace them. Tragically, if I believe a lie, I empower the liar. The enemy of our souls, satan works to trip us up through lies, intimidation, accusation, and seduction. His aim is to get us to question who God really is.

The devil's first interaction with Adam and Eve was to get them to question God's motives for giving a command not to eat the forbidden fruit, which was from the Tree of the Knowledge of Good and Evil. Satan said, *"You surely will not die! For God knows that in the day you eat from it your eyes will be opened, and you will be like God, knowing good and evil"* (Gen. 3:4-5). He accuses God of using His commands to protect Himself from humanity by keeping people from becoming like Him, knowing good and evil. Such nonsense was the tool used to poison humanity at its core.

Adam and Eve ate the forbidden fruit to become like God. They tried to obtain through an act what they already had by design—they were created in the image of God. They were already like Him! Jesus came as the Rescuer and crushed the serpent's head (see Genesis 3:15).

● ● ●

PRAYER

Lord, You are the One who rescues me from falsehood.
I get to see You move on my behalf again and again.

THIRTY DAYS

REFLECTIONS ON THE GOODNESS OF GOD

THE BETTER COVENANT

BUT NOW HE HAS OBTAINED A MORE EXCELLENT
MINISTRY, INASMUCH AS HE IS ALSO
MEDIATOR OF A BETTER COVENANT, WHICH
WAS ESTABLISHED ON BETTER PROMISES.
—HEBREWS 8:6

The Lord gave the earth to the children of men (Psalm 115:16). This highest of honors was given to us because love always chooses the best. That is the beginning of the romance of our creation—created in His image, for intimacy, that dominion might be expressed through love. It is from this revelation that we are to learn to walk as His ambassadors, thus defeating the "prince of this world" (see John 14:30, Eph. 2:2).

The Gospel of salvation is to touch the whole man: spirit, soul, and body. John G. Lake called this a Triune Salvation. A study on the word evil confirms the intended reach of His redemption. When Matthew 6:13 says, *"Deliver us from evil"* (KJV), the word evil represents the entire curse of sin upon man. Poneros, the Greek word for "evil," came from the word ponos, meaning "pain."

And that word came from the root word penes, meaning "poor." Look at it:

- Evil: sin
- Pain: sickness
- Poor: poverty

Jesus destroyed the power of sin, sickness, and poverty through His redemptive work on the cross. In Adam and Eve's commission to subdue the earth, they were without sin, sickness, and poverty. Now that we are restored to His original purpose, should we expect anything less? After all, this is called the better covenant!

● ● ●

PRAYER

Father, thank You for all You have done to bring me out of darkness and into Your glorious light. Thank You that You created me in Your image, for intimacy.

THE BEAUTY OF THE OLD TESTAMENT

ALL SCRIPTURE IS GIVEN BY INSPIRATION
OF GOD, AND IS PROFITABLE FOR DOCTRINE,
FOR REPROOF, FOR CORRECTION, FOR
INSTRUCTION IN RIGHTEOUSNESS.

—2 TIMOTHY 3:16

I remember growing up thinking that God the Father was angry, and it was Jesus who calmed Him down. The stories of the Old Testament only seemed to confirm that misguided idea. It almost seemed like there were two completely different deities in charge of each dispensation.

While that is not true, we've been left with a challenging task of reconciling the unique approaches to problems that couldn't be more diametrically opposed to each other than they are in the Old and New Testaments. And while there are glimpses of grace in the Old, it is the ongoing judgments, diseases, curses, and the like that all seem to have God's blessing, that become a theological nightmare—at least for me. I will admit that many people seem to have no problem with the conflict, but in all honesty, I refuse to embrace their theology. For the most part their concept of God violates all that Jesus Christ stood for and modeled for us to follow. Discovering the role of the Old Testament in the days of the New Testament is absolutely needed so that we might live in wisdom.

●　●　●

PRAYER

Lord, Your song is in my heart. I carry the song of my Father.

A RICH RESOURCE

"BLESSED SHALL YOU BE WHEN YOU COME IN,
AND BLESSED SHALL YOU BE WHEN YOU GO OUT."
—DEUTERONOMY 28:6

I absolutely love all of Scripture, and I have a special fondness for the Old Testament. If you can read and embrace it without being offended at God or using it to replace the standard that Jesus set in the New Testament, then it becomes a most glorious journey. Old Covenant Scripture remains a rich resource for the instruction of the New Testament believer.

I realize that it is impossible to fully describe the beauty, wonder, and purpose of the Old Testament in such a small book. But hopefully, the following will help you to understand the high points of the Lord's targets in inspiring such wonder as the writing of Old Covenant Scripture. Here are four of the main things that the Old Testament does for us that are helpful in recognizing and living in the goodness of God. The Old Testament reveals the severity of sin, exposes the absolute hopeless condition of humanity to save itself, shows us our need of a savior, and points to Jesus as the only possible solution to our lost condition. In other words, it carries the story of hope.

● ● ●

Prayer

Lord, You have done so much to help me see Your goodness. Thank You for the way You seek out my heart.

FORGIVENESS UNTO ADOPTION

WHERE THERE IS NO LAW THERE
IS NO TRANSGRESSION.

—ROMANS 4:15

God does nothing to create shame in us. All that He reveals to us He does out of His goodness so that we might respond to His provision and become free. Sin is so severe it is terminal in every single case. It cannot be overlooked. The presence and power of sin have scarred all that God has made. No one can survive the effects of sin.

The Law illustrates how sin contaminates everything it touches. If you touch a leper in the Old Testament, you are unclean, requiring a process to become clean again. If you are bringing a lamb to be sacrificed, and somebody spits on it, the offering is now unclean. The idea is driven home page after page as the severity of sin must be realized to effectively turn from it unto God.

The point is, under the Old Covenant unclean things affect the clean things. Sin contaminates. Without knowing our need, it's impossible to recognize His answer. When He reveals our absolute lost condition because of sin, He does so that we might turn from sin and receive His solution—forgiveness unto adoption.

* * *

PRAYER

Lord, You have made me Your child. This is my true state, and it will not change.

DAY 35

HE IS OUR HOPE

HE BROUGHT THEM OUT OF DARKNESS
AND THE SHADOW OF DEATH, AND
BROKE THEIR CHAINS IN PIECES.
—PSALM 107:14

The Old Testament gives us an awareness of our
sinfulness, revealing that we can't just decide not
to sin anymore. Sinfulness has become our nature. No
amount of discipline or determination can change our
bent toward sin, nor can it rid us of our sinful past.

One of the more sobering realizations is that there is
no number of good works that can make up for our sins.
Self-help programs might help with losing weight or learning new skills, but they cannot touch the human dilemma
called sin. It is out of the reach of all human efforts. Seeing
that we are lost—completely lost—opens us up to outside
help. And that outside help is from God Himself. We
realize our need for a savior. The stubborn insistence that
we must provide for ourselves and take care of ourselves

might help in some parts of life, but it is completely useless as it pertains to our need of salvation. Because we are lost, we must be found. The stage is set for the Savior.

●　●　●

PRAYER

Father, You sought me out and gave me mercy when I did not deserve it. And so began my life, renewed and fully accepted as Your child.

THE OLD TESTAMENT IS A TEACHER

THEREFORE THE LAW HAS BECOME OUR TUTOR
TO LEAD US TO CHRIST, SO THAT WE MAY BE
JUSTIFIED BY FAITH. BUT NOW THAT FAITH HAS
COME, WE ARE NO LONGER UNDER A TUTOR.
—GALATIANS 3:24-25

In reality, none of us can "find Jesus." The Bible describes us as dead (separate from God). And dead people can't find a savior. Strangely, this provides the backdrop for all of us, as it pertains to our salvation. Those who are seeking God are simply responding to the summons of God that has been released over their hearts. We were found. Jesus called us by name, bringing conviction of sin into our lives. We responded and were born again—we came to life.

The Old Testament Law is the teacher that leads us to Christ. It first reveals that we are sinners, but thankfully, it doesn't leave us there. Jesus not only satisfied the appetite of the Law in bearing our judgment upon Himself;

He was the One the Law was pointing to, much like a sign on a restaurant points to what's inside the building. The Mosaic Law pointed to Jesus.

As you read and reread Old Testament Scriptures, it becomes obvious that the Father wanted us to realize that His answer was on the way. The Savior was on the way.

• • •

PRAYER

Father, I want to see Your truth even in books of the Bible I have never been able to understand. Teach me Your ways so I can know You.

WHAT DOES THE KINGDOM LOOK LIKE?

NOW WHEN HE WAS ASKED BY THE PHARISEES
WHEN THE KINGDOM OF GOD WOULD COME, HE
ANSWERED THEM AND SAID, "THE KINGDOM OF
GOD DOES NOT COME WITH OBSERVATION; NOR
WILL THEY SAY, 'SEE HERE!' OR 'SEE THERE!' FOR
INDEED, THE KINGDOM OF GOD IS WITHIN YOU."
—LUKE 17:20-21

Because the Old Testament leads us to Jesus, it automatically points to the Kingdom that this King of kings rules over. The Kingdom is the realm of His rule, displaying His will for all He has made. Page after page of the Old Testament carries the wonderful picture of the Kingdom of God that was to come. Throughout the time before Christ, there were events, prophecies, and laws that spoke of life under grace. There were unusual moments of grace that gave insight into what was coming through types and shadows.

And while Israel expected the Kingdom to show up through the military rule of their Messiah, Jesus revealed it as a Kingdom that first touched the heart. The very word for salvation was never meant to mean "forgiveness of sin" alone. It is a word that means "wholeness, forgiveness, healing, and deliverance." Look at the Romans passage about the Kingdom—righteousness, peace, and joy (see Rom. 14:17). Righteousness deals with the sin issue, peace answers the deliverance/torment issue, and joy is the answer for sickness and disease. "Laughter is good medicine" (see Prov. 17:22). A healthy inward lifestyle affects our health, finances, and our overall well-being (3 John 2). The Kingdom of God is within us.

● ● ●

PRAYER

Father, You are good! Your life flows out of me like a river.

JOY UNSPEAKABLE

FOR THE KINGDOM OF GOD IS NOT EATING
AND DRINKING, BUT RIGHTEOUSNESS AND
PEACE AND JOY IN THE HOLY SPIRIT.
—ROMANS 14:17

The subject of God's goodness is one of the most obvious realities in existence. The stories of the Master's touch abound as person after person is healed and delivered by the love of this perfect Father. As strange as it may sound, none of the miracles of Jesus were given as a public relations move. In other words, they were not done to promote His ministry or to prove He had power. They all came out of His compassion for people, not to satisfy the need of onlookers for supernatural entertainment.

The Scriptures carry warnings for those who become mere observers of the supernatural without the change that can only happen through repentance. The Kingdom doesn't come to be measured outwardly, though it has a profound effect on things that are visible, like the healing and deliverance of the body (see Matt. 12:28). The Kingdom comes first to rule over and heal our hearts, and then to affect all things outwardly.

The Kingdom of God is not food or drink—outward things. Instead, it is entirely that which is unseen, in the heart—righteousness, peace, and joy. And while those things are inward issues, they quickly become manifest outwardly. It's hard to keep joy unseen.

●　●　●

PRAYER

Lord, I want to know Your name in a greater way. Help me to see the signs of Your name in my life.

THE NEW FULFILLS THE OLD

THE NEXT DAY JOHN SAW JESUS COMING TOWARD
HIM, AND SAID, "BEHOLD! THE LAMB OF GOD
WHO TAKES AWAY THE SIN OF THE WORLD!"
—JOHN 1:29

We can gain wonderful revelations about life under the New Covenant from the Old Testament's types and shadows.

For example, we know that the Jews were required to offer a spotless lamb as a payment for their sin. But we also know that Jesus is the actual Lamb of God who takes away the sin of the world. Once the actual comes in answer to the Old Testament type or shadow, there's no more need to go back and embrace the symbol. Otherwise, animal sacrifices would still have merit.

The entire Old Testament points to Jesus. He is the central figure of ALL Scripture. Both the Law and the Prophets declared His role as Messiah, showing how Jesus would fulfill God's redemptive plan. The stories, prophecies, and laws all pointed to Him at various levels in the same way that a highway sign points to an upcoming city from varying distances. The sign is real and significant, but in itself it is not the reality we are looking for. It points to something greater than itself. A freeway sign never defines the city, and neither should the Old Testament be made to redefine who Jesus is. Why did He come? He came to destroy the works of the devil.

● ● ●

PRAYER

Father, I carry Your light in a world filled with suffering. Thank You for the hope You have embedded within me that I can use to help others see Your truth.

THE NATURE OF THE MESSAGE

"THE LAW AND THE PROPHETS WERE UNTIL JOHN. SINCE THAT TIME THE KINGDOM OF GOD HAS BEEN PREACHED AND EVERYONE IS PRESSING INTO IT."
—LUKE 16:16

"Until John" is a significant phrase, but one that seems to be mostly ignored. Both the Law and the Prophets were trumped by a greater message, the Gospel of the Kingdom. One is the prevailing message while the other is obsolete, having been fulfilled. One has Heaven's backing; the other doesn't. One reveals God's purpose in this present day, defining our assignment; the other does not.

A message creates a reality. The nature of the message we carry determines the nature of the reality we will live and minister in. Those who fully embrace our God-given assignment for the message of the Kingdom will see the ever-increasing government of God displayed in the affairs of mankind. This is the only message that creates an environment suitable to the display of God's love, His uncompromising purity, and His unfathomable power. This is the message that Jesus preached and in turn taught His disciples to preach. It remains the now word.

The Kingdom is the message we're to carry forth into the nations of the world (see Matt. 10:7 and Acts 28:31). Our message is Jesus, who demonstrated what His world is like through words and actions.

● ● ●

Prayer

Lord, You are good! Thank You that You are with me, and I get to see You work in my life.

DAY 41

THE GOSPEL OF
THE KINGDOM

FOR OUR LIGHT AFFLICTION, WHICH IS BUT FOR
A MOMENT, IS WORKING FOR US A FAR MORE
EXCEEDING AND ETERNAL WEIGHT OF GLORY.
—2 CORINTHIANS 4:17

The Church has largely replaced the Gospel of the Kingdom with the Gospel of salvation. It's the beauty of the salvation message that makes it so easy to miss the fact that it is only a part of the whole message that Jesus gave us.

The Gospel of salvation is focused on getting people saved and going to Heaven. The Gospel of the Kingdom is focused on the transformation of lives, cities, and nations through the effect of God's present rule—this is made manifest by bringing the reality of Heaven to earth. We must not confuse our destiny with our assignment. Heaven is my destiny, while bringing the Kingdom is my assignment.

The focus of the Kingdom message is the rightful dominion of God over everything. Whatever is inconsistent with Heaven—namely, disease, torment, hatred, division, sin habits, etc.—must come under the authority of the King. These kinds of issues are broken off of people's lives because inferior realms cannot stand wherever the dominion of God becomes manifest.

As we succeed in displaying this message, we are positioned to bring about cultural change in education, business, politics, the environment, and the other essential issues that we face today.

● ● ●

PRAYER

Lord, You are better than I think. You are my answer and my hope.

WHEN HEAVEN WAS SILENT

"THE LAW AND THE PROPHETS WERE
UNTIL JOHN. SINCE THAT TIME THE
KINGDOM OF GOD HAS BEEN PREACHED
AND EVERYONE IS PRESSING INTO IT."
—LUKE 16:16

In Luke 16:16, why did Jesus say "until John" ? Wouldn't it have been better if He had said "until Jesus"? But John was the one who broke Heaven's silence with the message of the Kingdom. Before John the Baptist came on the scene, there were four hundred years without one word from God. Heaven was silent. No visions, dreams, or prophecies. Nothing. Four hundred years of absolute silence—and then came John.

The Holy Spirit is not carelessly highlighting this detail that the Law and the Prophets were until John because it was John who first declared, "Repent, for the kingdom of heaven is at hand!" (Matt. 3:2). John was the one who announced the shift in Heaven's focus.

There is another place in Scripture where four hundred years is unusually significant. Israel lived in Egypt as a nation of slaves for four hundred years. And then the divine moment came when everything changed. It was when the blood from a lamb was put on the door post of each Jewish home on the night specified by God. It is a new day. The new day is marked by a new message. One message is over, and another has begun.

● ● ●

PRAYER

Lord, You have given me exquisite freedom. You Yourself are my peace.

THE PRONOUNCEMENT THAT CHANGED EVERYTHING

THEREFORE, IF ANYONE IS IN CHRIST, HE IS
A NEW CREATION; OLD THINGS HAVE PASSED
AWAY; BEHOLD, ALL THINGS HAVE BECOME NEW.
—2 CORINTHIANS 5:17

The Angel of the Lord came and released Israel from their slavery in Egypt to their destiny as a Promised Land people. In one moment, they went from being slaves to being free, from absolute poverty to possessing the wealth of the most prosperous nation in the world. It happened in a moment. The first mention of the phrase four hundred years resulted in the rescue of a people and the formation of a nation, Israel. This was the redemption of God's people.

The time of John the Baptist marked the end of another four hundred years—four hundred years of silence. This time it would be a nation formed in the Spirit through conversion, including people from every tribe and tongue on the planet. For the first time since Genesis 1, there would actually be a "new creation" (see 2 Cor. 5:17), which is a people " born of the Spirit" (see John 3:6-8).

When John the Baptist appeared, it was even more significant than deliverance from four hundred years of slavery under Egypt. That deliverance dealt with the nature and potential of mankind, but John's pronouncement changed everything.

● ● ●

PRAYER

Lord, You have set me free from slavery. My heart knows how to sing because of Your goodness.

THE PROMISES OF GOD

"NOW THE KINGDOM OF GOD IS BEING PREACHED
AND EVERYONE IS PRESSING INTO IT."
—LUKE 16:16

Is it possible that the nature of the message determines the size of the harvest? Jesus did say "everyone" in Luke 16:16. While I do not believe in Universalism, where everyone eventually ends up in Heaven, the message of the Kingdom has a greater reach than I previously thought possible. This is the message: "His dominion is everlasting. It is NOW. Jesus' life demonstrated His dominion over everything that was inconsistent with God's will."

Don't skip over the bigger promises of Scripture simply because they are hard to believe because of their size. Whenever He declares something this big, He's hoping to capture people's hearts, making it impossible for them to be satisfied with mediocrity. In Joel 2:28, He says, *"I will pour out My Spirit on all flesh."* In Jeremiah 31:34, He states, *"And all shall know Me."* Psalm 22, the psalm that deals with the crucifixion of Christ more than any other, states, *"All the ends of the world shall remember and turn to the Lord, and all the families of the nations shall worship before You"* (Ps. 22:27).

This list of extraordinary promises could continue page after page. But you get the point. The promises are there, in a sense waiting for adoption.

● ● ●

PRAYER

Father, You have never forsaken Your promises to me. Thank You that I get to see You move mightily in my life and in the lives of my family members.

THE BIGGER PROMISES OF SCRIPTURE

ALL THE ENDS OF THE WORLD SHALL REMEMBER
AND TURN TO THE LORD, AND ALL THE FAMILIES
OF THE NATIONS SHALL WORSHIP BEFORE YOU.
—PSALM 22:27

How many times did the disciples get the timing right in their understanding of God's prophetic promises? I don't consider myself any better than they were. The bigger promises are not given to us to help us to know the future as much as they are given to create hunger for what might be. The promises of God are clearly seen when the people of God get hungry and cry out to God for their fulfillment. This is exactly what Daniel did in reading Jeremiah's prophecy (see Dan. 9:2-6). He turned the prophecies into prayers for his generation.

When you declare the right message, you create the atmosphere where everyone is able to press in. No matter the need, there is an answer now. The right message marries the truth of Jesus as the desire of the nations with the nations themselves. The right message changes the atmosphere to make the manifestation of His dominion realized. Perhaps this is the context in which the irresistible grace of God is embraced, thus fulfilling the desire found in the heart of every person alive.

● ● ●

PRAYER

Lord, I want to show who You are to the people in my life. Help me to reveal Your heart and nature clearly.

IT IS FINISHED

AFTER THIS, JESUS, KNOWING THAT ALL
THINGS WERE NOW ACCOMPLISHED, THAT THE
SCRIPTURE MIGHT BE FULFILLED, SAID, "I
THIRST!" ...SO WHEN JESUS HAD RECEIVED THE
SOUR WINE, HE SAID, "IT IS FINISHED!" AND
BOWING HIS HEAD, HE GAVE UP HIS SPIRIT.
—JOHN 19:28-30

It is a mistake to think that when Jesus cried out, "It is finished." He was merely proclaiming that His life as a man living on earth was over. Both the Law and the Prophets had rightfully made a judgment on humanity, for God Himself declared, *"The person who sins shall die!"* (Ezek. 18:20). The power of this judgment was so strong that if Jesus had not come for one hundred thousand years, and trillions of people had lived during that time, it rightfully would have damned every single one and still not have been satisfied in its demands.

Jesus came to quench the appetite of that unquench-able fire by meeting the requirements of the Law and the

Prophets. When He said, "It is finished," He was declaring, "The appetite of the Law and Prophets has been satisfied once and for all! It's a new day."

As a result, we each go from a slave to a possessor of the Kingdom in a moment: transferred from the kingdom of darkness to the Kingdom of light, from being the one who has no rights in God to suddenly being the eternal dwelling place of God Himself.

● ● ●

PRAYER

Thank You, Father, for Your peace. Thank You that You know exactly what my heart needs at any given time.

IT ISN'T COMPLICATED

"REPENT, FOR THE KINGDOM OF
HEAVEN IS AT HAND."
—MATTHEW 4:17

This word "repent" means "to change our way of thinking." But it is much more than a mental exercise. It really is the deep sorrow for sin that enables a person to truly repent and change his mind or perspective on reality. Hebrews 6:1 clearly teaches that there are two sides to this action: *"Repentance from dead works...faith toward God."*

Full repentance is from something toward something—from sin toward God. Many Christians repent enough to be forgiven but not enough to see the Kingdom. Their repentance doesn't bring the Kingdom into view.

The same concept is taught with two different perspectives. One passage (Hebrews 6:1) says *"toward God"* and the other (Matthew 4:17) implies it's *"toward the Kingdom."* Luke captures the richness of both views when he writes: *"Repent therefore and be converted, that your sins may be blotted out, so that times of refreshing may come from the presence of the Lord"* (Acts 3:19).

The point is the presence is the Kingdom. It really is that simple. It's too easy to complicate the Christian life.

●　●　●

PRAYER

Lord, wherever my thoughts do not look like Your thoughts, I want to change. Help me to see Your truth.

THE ARMOR OF GOD

HE SHALL COME DOWN LIKE RAIN UPON
THE GRASS BEFORE MOWING, LIKE
SHOWERS THAT WATER THE EARTH.
—PSALM 72:6

There is no sickness in Heaven. When the Kingdom is manifest in a person's body, he is healed (see Matt. 4:23). There are no demons in Heaven, which is why deliverance is normal when Jesus touches people (see Matt. 12:28). It's all about what His world looks like, and how that reality can affect this one.

We are told to put on the full armor of God, which includes the helmet of salvation, breastplate of righteousness, and so on (see Eph. 6:10-18). The apostle Paul gave us this important instruction, but most of the time we miss the point. God is my armor. He's not saying, "Put something on that is a reality that is separate from Me." He's saying, "I'm it. Just abide in Me. I become your salvation. I am your righteousness, the breastplate over you.

I am the Gospel of peace. I am the Good News. I am the sword of the Spirit." This list paints a profound word picture, enabling us to realize the fuller benefit of abiding in Christ. Simple is better.

Jesus tells us to repent because He brought His world with Him. Discovering the presence of God is discovering the Kingdom.

● ● ●

PRAYER

Father, You are my hiding place. Teach me how to abide in You, even in the midst of everyday life.

THE OLD HAS A PURPOSE

FOR WHATEVER WAS WRITTEN IN EARLIER
TIMES WAS WRITTEN FOR OUR INSTRUCTION,
SO THAT THROUGH PERSEVERANCE
AND THE ENCOURAGEMENT OF THE
SCRIPTURES WE MIGHT HAVE HOPE.

—ROMANS 15:4

I love the Bible, the whole Bible, more than I have words to express. My personal study of the Scriptures has been spent in both the Old and New Testaments. I spent many years teaching primarily from the Old Testament Scriptures, as I discovered that they were the "root system" for what we enjoy in Christ. It was an essential part of my developing years. Seeing the purposes of God as revealed in His dealings with Israel and the surrounding nations has proven to be invaluable for me as I consider His design and purpose for the New Testament Church. It's been a glorious journey, one that continues to develop in beauty and purpose.

Romans 15:4 addresses the purpose of studying the Old Testament. The correct study of Scripture is to give us encouragement that results in great hope—that we might have hope. And yet for many, the study of the Old Testament does anything but give them hope for their own lives. All many see are the judgments of God toward the nations. I believe if we get a different outcome than what this Romans passage said we would have (encouragement and hope), we must learn to approach the Scriptures differently until we bear His intended fruit.

● ● ●

PRAYER

Father, I love the story You are telling with Your Word. I ask that I would be able to see the secrets about You and what You are doing contained within Scripture.

THE ONLY BIBLE THE CHURCH HAD

*FOR THE LETTER KILLS, BUT
THE SPIRIT GIVES LIFE.*
—2 CORINTHIANS 3:6

The Old Testament was given for our instruction as New Covenant people. For a season the Old Testament Scriptures were the only Bible the New Testament Church had. What has been written gives us the backdrop to the truths we enjoy today. But as it is with most things, improper application can also bring death (see 2 Cor. 3:6).

It's a matter of perception. Many Christians' lives have been crippled because of an unclear understanding of what Jesus came to accomplish and fulfill. If I don't understand that, I won't understand my purpose and calling. To put it more practically, through wisdom and revelation we must understand what of the Old Testament ended at the cross, what was changed by the cross, and what came through the cross unchanged.

So many believers live under the curse of the Law because of taking the wrong approach to the Old Testament. This simple adjustment will help us live in the freedom that Jesus bought for us. For in living in freedom, we illustrate what He is like and model what living under His rule looks like. This is a huge part of our message of the Gospel—live it, and when necessary use words.

● ● ●

PRAYER

Your holiness is more powerful than any darkness. Thank You that I get to go out into the world and reveal the Father, just as Jesus did.

WHAT ENDED AT THE CROSS

FOR AS BY ONE MAN'S DISOBEDIENCE MANY
WERE MADE SINNERS, SO ALSO BY ONE MAN'S
OBEDIENCE MANY WILL BE MADE RIGHTEOUS.
—ROMANS 5:19

The sacrifice of animals was required under the Old Testament Law. It was mandated by God to remind us that the penalty of sin is death. And while the blood of animals never actually did away with the record of sin, dealt with the nature of sin in the ones making the sacrifice, or dealt with the consequences of sin, it did postpone the penalty for one more year. It became a point of obedience that prophesied of what was coming—the Lamb of God, who would take away the sins of the world.

When Jesus offered Himself as a sacrifice on behalf of all mankind, He made it possible for the sacrifice of one to make the many righteous. His death on our behalf changed everything. He was the Lamb of God, without sin, blemish, or fault of any kind. The requirement of the

Law for the shedding of blood for sin was satisfied for all time.

The cross brought an end to the sacrifice of animals and, more importantly, satisfied the appetite of the Law for the judgment of humanity. Salvation is now given to all who call upon the name of the Lord.

● ● ●

PRAYER

You have shown me mercy. You've wiped away my sin and brought me home.

SALVATION WITHOUT WORKS

AND HE SAID TO THEM, "THE
SABBATH WAS MADE FOR MAN, AND
NOT MAN FOR THE SABBATH."
—MARK 2:27

The Sabbath was created for the benefit of mankind. It was an important enough part of God's economy that He Himself rested the seventh day from His works in creation.

On the Sabbath, the seventh day, we are to rest from all our labors. God even required that the land rest every seven years (rest from planting crops). Then every seventh Sabbath year required yet another year of rest, this time marked by what the Bible calls the Year of Jubilee. So that means that both the forty-ninth and the fiftieth year, the land rests again, while at the same time debts are forgiven, slaves are freed, and many other similar things are done to increase the well-being of God's people.

While I do think the weekly Sabbath rest is essential for mental, emotional, physical, and spiritual health, the Sabbath was also a foretaste of what the daily life of the believer is to be like—without works as it pertains to our salvation. When Jesus announced the beginning of His ministry, He declared, *"The Spirit of the Lord is upon Me...to declare the favorable year of the Lord"* (Luke 4:18). That year is the Year of Jubilee! The Year of Jubilee is the ongoing experience of those belonging to Him.

● ● ●

PRAYER

Father, You are my jubilee. And You are also where I find my rest.

SABBATH FREEDOM FOR EVERY BELIEVER

NOW THE LORD IS THE SPIRIT, AND WHERE THE
SPIRIT OF THE LORD IS, THERE IS LIBERTY.
—2 CORINTHIANS 3:17

The Year of Jubilee was year the land rested, and God's people experienced another level of freedom: debts were forgiven, slaves were freed, and so forth. The freedom the Jubilee provides is to be the distinguishing mark on the lives of those who have met Jesus. Every day is the Sabbath and every year is the Year of Jubilee for us—rest and liberty are to be seen on the countenance of all who belong to Him. While I don't think there are many who truly live the beauty of this truth, it is a reality of His Kingdom that is available to all.

Both the Sabbath and the Jubilee were changed through the sacrifice of Jesus on our behalf. The cross changed the nature of rest and freedom. Instead of happening every fifty years, Jubilee is now the everyday lifestyle of those in Christ.

The Old Testament is filled with things that were prototypes, or prophetic glimpses of the future. And all of these things reveal layer after layer of the goodness of God that was to become more fully manifest on this side of the cross.

• • •

Prayer

Father, help me to understand the depths of the freedom You offer me in Jesus. My entire life needs the freedom You offer.

WE WANT THE FACE OF GOD

"FOR HOW THEN WILL IT BE KNOWN THAT
YOUR PEOPLE AND I HAVE FOUND GRACE
IN YOUR SIGHT, EXCEPT YOU GO WITH US?
SO WE SHALL BE SEPARATE, YOUR PEOPLE
AND I, FROM ALL THE PEOPLE WHO ARE
UPON THE FACE OF THE EARTH."
—EXODUS 33:16

King David is known for many wonderful things throughout Scripture. He was a great king who led Israel into their greatest hour. He was a man after God's heart, which he proved long before He became king. His courage against the lion and the bear when no one was watching set him up for the victory over Goliath when two entire nations were watching. This set the pace for His profound leadership with the people of God—one of extraordinary courage.

But the primary reference point in all his life was his passion for the presence of God. It was his worship that sculpted the heart of a nation, turning them into a people who valued the presence of God. As Moses once declared, it was the presence of God upon His people that became the distinguishing mark that separated them from all other nations. Under David's leadership, the priests turned from the focus of keeping the Law to keeping the presence. An important feature to remember is that most of the time when the Bible talks about the presence of God, it's actually talking about His face. That is the meaning of the Hebrew word translated presence.

● ● ●

PRAYER

You are the One who heals me. I find rest in Your presence and joy in Your smile.

A NEW TESTAMENT REALITY

WHEN YOU SAID, "SEEK MY FACE," MY HEART
SAID TO YOU, "YOUR FACE, LORD, I WILL SEEK."
—PSALM 27:8

David was a worshiper on the backside of the desert caring for his father's sheep. This wasn't done for performance or status. It was the purest expression of his heart and became the reason for God choosing him above his brothers as the ruler over Israel. When David became king, he wanted the Ark of the Covenant, the dwelling place of God among mankind, in his city of Jerusalem. So David pitched a tent on Mount Zion that housed the Ark of the Covenant.

We don't know the size of the tent. All we know is that God was there, and so were the priests. They ministered to God through thanksgiving, praise, and worship with their musical instruments and physical expressions like raising their hands, bowing low, dancing, as well as lifting up their voices.

The great honor for anyone, terrifying as it may have been, was to be able to come into the presence of the Almighty God. That very act was forbidden to them under the Law. But God in His mercy allowed them to taste of a New Testament reality long before its time. Under David, they did this daily. We now have the privilege of ministering to God as they did in David's tabernacle.

● ● ●

Prayer

You are my God, and You have taught me of Your goodness. Your presence is my delight.

WORSHIP AND EVANGELISM

AND THOSE OF THE CIRCUMCISION WHO
BELIEVED WERE ASTONISHED, AS MANY
AS CAME WITH PETER, BECAUSE THE
GIFT OF THE HOLY SPIRIT HAD BEEN
POURED OUT ON THE GENTILES ALSO.

—ACTS 10:45

The prophet Amos declared that in the last days there would be a rebuilding of the Tabernacle of David. This was the tent David set up for the Ark of the Covenant on Mount Zion. It was known for the abiding presence of God and the priests' worship. The time of the word's fulfillment would be when the Gentiles were added to what God was doing on the earth. They, too, would become His people (see Amos 9:11-12).

And that is what happened. After Jesus gave the Great Commission to the Church to *"go into all the world"* (Matt. 28:19), followed by the outpouring of the Holy Spirit that would help them be effective (see Acts 2), Gentiles began to be added to the Church. The rebuilding of this tabernacle coincides with Gentiles being added to the faith. The Tabernacle of David changed the focus of life and ministry for all priests in the Old Testament. They had to shift their focus from the sacrifice of animals to the sacrifice of praise. In the New Testament, we discover that every believer is now a priest unto the Lord (see 1 Pet. 2:9). There is a connection in the unseen realm between the effect of worship and the conversion of souls.

● ● ●

PRAYER

Lord, You have been so good to me. I pray that through my life and worship, Your goodness would draw people to You.

HIS GOODNESS, HIS GLORY

THE LORD IS NOT SLACK CONCERNING
HIS PROMISE, AS SOME COUNT SLACKNESS,
BUT IS LONGSUFFERING TOWARD US, NOT
WILLING THAT ANY SHOULD PERISH BUT
THAT ALL SHOULD COME TO REPENTANCE.

—2 PETER 3:9

The Law of Moses was but for a season. It was never meant to carry the full manifestation of God's nature to be discovered and enjoyed by His people. While it was necessary and beautiful, it fell far short in representing the Father's heart. That was not its purpose.

The Law taught Israel what they needed to know about the Messiah before He came upon the scene. Riddled all throughout God's dealings with His people in the Old Testament was the revelation of grace. Some of the most beautiful glimpses of God's heart are hidden in the scenes of the Old Testament.

God illustrated His heart for His people over and over again. He declared, *"Say to them, 'As I live!' declares the*

Lord God, 'I take no pleasure in the death of the wicked, but rather that the wicked turn from his way and live'" (Ezek. 33:11). God is not an angry tyrant wishing evil people to be punished and die. His passion for all of us is to experience life to the fullest! But it is never forced upon us; otherwise, He ends up with robots, not people made in His image.

●   ●   ●

PRAYER

Father, help me to see Your heart clearly. I want to represent You well to the people around me.

SPOKEN BLESSINGS

"THE LORD BLESS YOU, AND KEEP YOU; THE
LORD MAKE HIS FACE SHINE ON YOU, AND BE
GRACIOUS TO YOU; THE LORD LIFT UP HIS
COUNTENANCE ON YOU, AND GIVE YOU PEACE."
—NUMBERS 6:24-26

One of the most treasured portions of Old Testament Scripture is the blessing God told Moses to pass on to Aaron to declare over His people. Obviously, God can bless whomever He wants, whenever He wants. But He longed for His people to know His heart for them. He also wanted it to be spoken, as something happens when we join our words with His heart.

Aaron was the high priest, and as such he was positioned to release the blessing of God over the people. God wanted blessing declared over His people every day of their lives. It was to be declared because what is spoken makes a difference. This was not simply a formality. Everything God tells us to do has great significance. This is a picture of the high priest joining his heart with the heart of God—to release the reality of His Kingdom into the lives of His people through decree.

We live with the conviction that nothing happens in the Kingdom of God until something is spoken. Numbers 6:22-27 reveals His passion for His people to know of His love, His bounty, and His all sufficiency. It is the heart of God for us all.

● ● ●

PRAYER

Father, I want to know Your heart for me. Thank You that it is a heart of blessing.

THE GOD JOURNEY

"HE WHO HAS MY COMMANDMENTS AND KEEPS THEM, IT IS HE WHO LOVES ME. AND HE WHO LOVES ME WILL BE LOVED BY MY FATHER, AND I WILL LOVE HIM AND MANIFEST MYSELF TO HIM."
—JOHN 14:21

God invites us to discover Him, the One who rewards all who join in the journey into the great expanse called the goodness of God. This is the journey of faith, for faith believes *that He is, and that He is the rewarder of those who seek Him* (Heb. 11:6).

Faith has two parts; the first is a conviction of His existence. But even the devil has that much going for him. It's the second part that launches us into the adventure and distinguishes us from the rest of all that exists—a confidence in His nature. He is a rewarder! In other words, what we believe about Him will have an effect on our lives in a measurable way because He rewards those who have set their hearts on discovering Him. He promises, *"You will seek Me...and I will be found by you!"* (Jer. 29:13-14).

God ensures that we find Him if the heart is genuinely searching with a readiness to obey. Jesus also said He would disclose Himself to those who follow Him. It's as though He is saying that if we seek Him with all of our hearts, He will make sure to put Himself in the middle of the road we're walking on.

● ● ●

PRAYER

Lord, I want to know You. I want to see Your face. Thank You that You want to be found.

A JOURNEY OF FAITH

BY FAITH WE UNDERSTAND THAT THE
WORLDS WERE PREPARED BY THE WORD OF
GOD, SO THAT WHAT IS SEEN WAS NOT MADE
OUT OF THINGS WHICH ARE VISIBLE.
—HEBREWS 11:3

The greatest gift we could ever give ourselves is to anchor our intellect and will into the strongest foundation possible—the goodness of God. This voyage is one of faith. Faith is considered to be anti-intellectual by many. It is not. In reality, it enhances the intellect but is vastly superior, for it is able to recognize the unseen world that the natural mind has little place for. Real faith is superior to the human intellect in that it is the product of God's mind instead of ours. Faith comes from the heart, one that lives under the influence of His mind.

Faith is the result of surrender, not self-will. It's more correctly stated that our intellect is shaped and influenced by authentic faith, for true faith precedes understanding on eternal matters, like those pertaining to the unseen world. It is faith that enables us to understand the unseen world, which according to the apostle Paul is eternal, while the things we see are temporal (see 2 Cor. 4:18). So faith then anchors us into the substance of eternity, a solid footing for sure. By faith we understand, for it is faith that enhances the intellect.

* * *

PRAYER

Lord, I get to be with You even in the processes of my mind. My heart lives under the influence of Your mind.

SIXTY DAYS

REFLECTIONS ON THE GOODNESS OF GOD

PEANUTS

"BUT LET HIM WHO GLORIES GLORY IN THIS,
THAT HE UNDERSTANDS AND KNOWS ME, THAT
I AM THE LORD, EXERCISING LOVINGKINDNESS,
JUDGMENT, AND RIGHTEOUSNESS IN THE EARTH.
FOR IN THESE I DELIGHT," SAYS THE LORD.
—JEREMIAH 9:24

History is filled with the stories of explorers and their adventures. We have been given the drive to search for more. God invites us into these quests as a part of our God-given nature to discover and create. His gifts of curiosity and desire are beautiful expressions of His heart as a Father.

George Washington Carver used this drive to discover things that would ultimately help the poor he lived to serve. His passion to unveil the secrets of creation began with his research on the peanut. He was known for his absolute faith in God as the cornerstone of his research and is credited with discovering over three hundred uses for the peanut. He claimed that it was faith that "held all inquiry and action accountable."[1] The impact of his research reached far and wide, but his primary target was to benefit the poor. As a result, this one man is credited with having an amazing impact on the economy of the southern states in the United States, all because he believed God rewards those who seek Him.

The Father draws us into the journey of discovering His nature. His entire realm of dominion called the Kingdom of God is hidden for us to find.

● ● ●

PRAYER

Lord, thank You that You are the God who desires to be found. Thank You that You're just waiting for me to seek You.

---

1. "Legacy of Dr. George Washington Carver: Scientist Extraordinaire, Man of Faith, Educator and Humanitarian," accessed 6 June 2016, http://www.tuskegee.edu/about_us/ legacy_of_fame/george_w_ carver.aspx.

GOD'S JOY IN YOUR SEARCH

IT IS THE GLORY OF GOD TO CONCEAL
A MATTER, BUT THE GLORY OF KINGS
IS TO SEARCH OUT A MATTER.

—PROVERBS 25:2

I find it fascinating that God is glorified by concealing or hiding things. But it must be understood that He hides things for us, not from us.

My wife Beni and I have nine grandchildren. On Easter we hide eggs for them in our front yard. While I've never been able to figure out what a bunny and eggs have to do with the resurrection of Jesus, we still love hiding eggs for the children in our lives. It is just another excuse to have fun with our family.

That being said, I would never dig a three-foot hole in the ground, put in the various kinds of eggs we use into the bottom of the hole, and then cover it with cement. Can you imagine me telling our grandchildren, "If you think you're so smart, try to find those eggs"? Hardly. We hide the eggs to be found. There's no joy in putting something out of their reach. Our joy is in their discovery.

This simple illustration wonderfully represents our discovery of God's goodness and speaks of His delight in our discovery. He truly is glorified in concealing a matter for us to find.

● ● ●

PRAYER

Father, You are the God who loves secret things and my discovery of them. Help me to see what You have hidden for me to find.

THE ROYALTY OF GOD'S PEOPLE

IT IS THE GLORY OF GOD TO CONCEAL
A MATTER, BUT THE GLORY OF KINGS
IS TO SEARCH OUT A MATTER.

—PROVERBS 25:2

The Father draws us into the journey of discovering His nature. His entire realm of dominion called the Kingdom of God is hidden for us to find. It is an eternal kingdom in which all of eternity will be needed to discover what He has made for us.

The second part of Proverbs 25:2 is equally important to the first part: "the glory of kings is to search out a matter." We have been created in the image of God, the King of all kings. We are royalty. Our royalty is never more at the forefront of our lives than when we live with the conviction that God has given us legal access to all things, including the hidden things—mysteries. And so we ask, seek, and knock, knowing there will be a breakthrough (see Matt. 7:7-8).

Some of the things in this kingdom are discovered almost without looking. They seem to find us. And yet other breakthroughs seem to take the better part of a lifetime. This joyful adventure begins now, but it will continue throughout all eternity. He rejoices as we discover His goodness.

● ● ●

PRAYER

You are my Father, who is absolutely good. I get to see Your goodness!

THE LAND OF GOODNESS

"SO I SAY TO YOU, ASK, AND IT WILL BE
GIVEN TO YOU; SEEK, AND YOU WILL FIND;
KNOCK, AND IT WILL BE OPENED TO YOU."
—LUKE 11:9

We are all explorers, searching for the new, enjoying the old, becoming personally enlarged with each discovery. What we behold affects us. If we look at it long enough, it changes us. There are parts of God's goodness that are easily noticeable to the casual observer. Much like Moses, we've been given a challenge. He saw a burning bush that wasn't being consumed by its flames. The story records an important detail that should help us all in our journey. It was only when Moses turned aside that the Lord spoke to him from the bush (see Exod. 3:4).

Sometimes giving undivided attention to the obvious releases a greater encounter with Him, manifesting a greater revelation of what He is like. The bottom line is that we can't find anything significant on our own. It must be revealed to us. In other words, all discoveries are not the result of our discipline and determination alone. As the ultimate steward, He gives these gifts to those who have embraced His invitation to ask, seek, and knock.

Prayer: Lord, help me to see Your goodness in my everyday life. Help me to stop, turn, and see, the way Moses did.

● ● ●

PRAYER

You have revealed Your goodness to me, and I love it. I look forward to exploring this vast territory of Your goodness for years to come.

CALL UPON ME

"CALL TO ME AND I WILL ANSWER YOU,
AND I WILL TELL YOU GREAT AND MIGHTY
THINGS, WHICH YOU DO NOT KNOW."
—JEREMIAH 33:3

Those of us who seek Him will find Him. The prophet Jeremiah caught a glimpse of this reality when God gave him a promise of restoration in Jeremiah 33. The God who is good gave us the invitation to call upon Him. He then promised to answer in a way that was beyond what we asked for.

The word *great* in Jeremiah 33:3 means "considerably above average." And if that weren't enough, He follows the word great with the word mighty. Mighty means "inaccessible." Consider this: God has given us access to the inaccessible. What an incomprehensible promise! It is out of the reach of our skills, character, or qualifications. We lack all that is necessary to be able to apprehend what exists in the realm called the goodness of God. But He gave us something that makes this impossibility possible. He gave us the key to the inaccessible. He Himself is that key.

Through His name we have access to that which is beyond our reach on our best day. The invitation came from His goodness. He invites us to call upon Him, giving Him the open door to answer in a way that is above our expectations and imagination.

● ● ●

PRAYER

You hear every prayer I pray. My voice is sacred to You. You treasure it.

They Want to Believe God Is Good

MOSES DID NOT KNOW THAT THE
SKIN OF HIS FACE SHONE BECAUSE
OF HIS SPEAKING WITH HIM.

—EXODUS 34:30

The Law was given to Moses. However, in one of his encounters with God, we see an example of grace that creates a high watermark, even by New Testament standards. The apostle Paul mentioned it in Second Corinthians 3:7-18, announcing that this glorious moment was less than what the New Covenant provided for each believer. The New Covenant is better than the Old, and therefore must provide superior blessings and breakthroughs.

In Exodus 33, Moses asked to see God's glory. God said, "Okay," and showed Moses His goodness. Take note! It was His goodness that changed Moses' countenance. This, the one time Moses' own countenance was changed, was only after a fresh revelation of God's goodness.

Is it possible that God intends to change the countenance of His people by a fresh revelation of His goodness? I think so. The world has seen a divided Church, an angry Church, a materialistic Church, and the list goes on. What would happen if they were to see a Church whose very countenance has been transformed by seeing Him, His glory—His goodness? This is what the world is crying for; they want to believe it's true—God is good. How we behold Him is what makes this a possibility.

●　●　●

Prayer

Lord, Your goodness changes me. I have been transformed by Your glory. Help me to see Your goodness more and more clearly.

A FRIEND OF GOD

THE LORD USED TO SPEAK TO MOSES FACE TO
FACE, JUST AS A MAN SPEAKS TO HIS FRIEND.
—EXODUS 33:11

In Exodus 33, Moses asked God not to send an angel
with Israel into the Promised Land—He wanted
God Himself to go. In fact, Moses stated that if God
wasn't going to go, then he didn't want to go either. This
really is quite remarkable. The angel assigned to lead
them would have provided everything God promised.
It would have been a fulfillment of all their dreams and
aspirations as a nation. And I remind you that angels
carry a certain majesty and glory that is often mistaken
for God Himself.

Yet Moses had a relationship with God, forged
through his trials. As a friend of God, Moses wanted only
to be led by his friend. The blessings were not the objec-
tive. The relationship was. And God replied to Moses'
request, *"I will also do this thing of which you have spoken;*

for you have found favor in My sight and I have known you by name" (Exodus 33:17).

This encounter with God occurred under the Old Covenant. We are now living in the New Covenant, which is better than the Old. There are great differences between law and grace, but for now, this will suffice: law requires, while grace enables.

●　●　●

PRAYER

Father, Your grace enables me. Like Moses, please guide me. I just want to be led by my Friend.

THE SACRIFICE OF PRAISE

THEREFORE BY HIM LET US CONTINUALLY
OFFER THE SACRIFICE OF PRAISE TO
GOD, THAT IS, THE FRUIT OF OUR LIPS,
GIVING THANKS TO HIS NAME.
—HEBREWS 13:15

Ever since my dad taught us what it means to be a priest unto the Lord, ministering to Him with our thanksgiving, praise, and worship, I have embraced this as a primary purpose for my life. Every time I read in Scripture that there are people ministering to Him and then there's a response from Heaven, I get excited. The lessons are always profound, as there's something of eternity on those moments.

In 2 Chronicles 5:13-14, the priests gave the fruit of the lips as their offering, and the house of the Lord filled with the cloud of His presence. While this happened in the Old Testament, it is clearly a New Testament practice, as the Law required the sacrifice of animals from the priests, not praise.

The priests were in unity as they praised God. Scripture says they were "as one." Remember that the 120 believers in Acts 1-2 were also in unity before the outpouring of the Holy Spirit took place. God loves to manifest Himself upon His people when we're known for our love of each other. He puts His glory upon a united people (see Ps. 133).

● ● ●

PRAYER

Father, I praise You for your goodness. I have seen You in my life, and I look forward to Your faithfulness in every promise.

THE GLORY OF GOD

"FOR HE IS GOOD, FOR HIS MERCY
ENDURES FOREVER."
—2 CHRONICLES 5:13

When the priests praised God for His goodness, His glory filled His house (see 2 Chron. 5:13-14). They declared the Lord to be good! He was not ashamed to put His glory upon and in the physical buildings that people built in honor of His name. How much more will He put the glory in the house that He Himself builds?

Once again we see a connection between the revelation of His goodness and His glory—His manifested presence. This is amazing, as the glory of God is to cover the earth as the waters cover the sea before time comes to an end (see Hab. 2:14). I suppose that many think this glory will become manifest through a military move of the return of the Messiah. But we often fail to understand the process He loves to work through. He longs for our involvement in all these matters. Co-laboring has been His heart from the beginning. And becoming a worshiping community that worships in spirit, in truth, and in unity will offer something to Him that He in turn will want to occupy— the praises of His people concerning His goodness.

● ● ●

PRAYER

May the knowledge of the glory of God spread to cover the earth. May the desires of Your heart come to pass.

DAY 70

THE HOUSE GOD BUILT

YOU ALSO, AS LIVING STONES, ARE BEING BUILT
UP A SPIRITUAL HOUSE, A HOLY PRIESTHOOD,
TO OFFER UP SPIRITUAL SACRIFICES
ACCEPTABLE TO GOD THROUGH JESUS CHRIST.
—1 PETER 2:5

If God did not hold back from putting His glory within physical temples, how much more will He put the glory in the house He builds Himself? And that house is the Church—the eternal dwelling place of God. (see Eph. 2:22). The Church is comprised of born-again believers who are as living stones, brought together into a spiritual house, to house a priesthood that will offer spiritual sacrifices, acceptable through Jesus. That is the revelation that Peter carried for us (see 1 Pet. 2:5). I remind you that many consider Peter to be the foundation of the ministry of the Church (see Matt. 16:18). And to take it one step further, the glory that is put within that house is to manifest the goodness of God, or we miss the point altogether.

I have this deep personal sense that the glory of God will be a primary subject and passion of the Church in the coming years.

● ● ●

PRAYER

Father, You have been so good to me, and Your love for me is everlasting. May Your glory become my passion.

DAY 71

THE HOPE OF GLORY

TO THEM GOD WILLED TO MAKE KNOWN
WHAT ARE THE RICHES OF THE GLORY OF
THIS MYSTERY AMONG THE GENTILES: WHICH
IS CHRIST IN YOU, THE HOPE OF GLORY.
— COLOSSIANS 1:27

The focus of the prophets, as well as the prophetic experiences contained throughout the Scriptures, oftentimes points to God's purposes for His people, the Church. The stories mentioned above reveal God's heart and plans for us. He has purposed to manifest Himself upon us and through us and, as a result, to transform the nature of the world around us. This must be seen, embraced, and received as a part of our reason for being.

The target of the Lord for us is still the glory. His glory is to become the dwelling place of God's people, as He in turn dwells in us. The apostle Paul used a phrase that is to grab our hearts: "Christ in you, the hope of glory." Jesus Christ in us makes it possible to be restored fully to His purpose for us—living in the glory. If the glory of God contains the revelation of the goodness of God, then here is a key. Jesus Christ dwelling in us by the Holy Spirit is what makes the revelation of His goodness known to and through us to the world around us. And that is hope illustrated.

● ● ●

PRAYER

Lord, I want to walk in Your purposes for me. Make the revelation of Your goodness known to me and through me!

GOD'S GLORY, OUR TARGET

AND HE SAID, "PLEASE, SHOW ME YOUR GLORY."
—EXODUS 33:18

When Moses asked to see the glory of God, he did not choose some random aspect of God's person or nature. He chose the original target for every person alive. We were created and designed to live in the glory of God, which is the manifested presence of Jesus.

The Scripture says, *"For all have sinned and fall short of the glory of God"* (Rom. 3:23). Sin caused us to fall short of God's intended target. To sin means "to miss the mark." Consider an archer shooting an arrow at a target and then watching that arrow not even reach the target, let alone hit the bull's-eye. That is what our sin has done. We not only missed the mark; we didn't even reach the target. But take note of the target—it is the glory of God. We were created to live in that realm. Moses knew it instinctively and longed to see it more clearly.

Many get stuck on the harshness of the Old Testament stories at the expense of seeing the reality of God's goodness that was displayed throughout history—much like a rose among thorns—but is now more fully manifest through the lifestyle illustrated by Jesus. It is, and has always been, about His goodness.

● ● ●

PRAYER

Lord, I want to see Your goodness in my life! Help me to be more aware of who You are and what You are doing in my everyday life.

Trusting in His Goodness

THEREFORE MY HEART IS GLAD, AND MY GLORY
REJOICES; MY FLESH ALSO WILL REST IN HOPE.
—PSALM 16:9

From my perspective, Psalm 27 is one of the most unusual and complete psalms in the Bible. It's a personal favorite. And as such, it has been a wonderful feeding place for my soul for many years. The writer illustrates his absolute trust in God (verses 1-3), the supreme value for His presence (verses 4-6), and his own devotion to obedience (verses 7-10). But the grand finale is the unveiling of his personal secret to strength (verses 11-14). He writes, "I would have despaired unless I had believed that I would see the goodness of the Lord in the land of the living." It was his hope of seeing the goodness of God in his day that kept him from hopelessness.

Hopelessness is a thief, one that is often welcomed into Christian circles in the name of discernment. This deceptive influence must be marked and recognized as a tool of the enemy. If ever there was a season in all of history that the people of God need to believe we'll see the glory of God, it is now. God's people are to be known for their hope, regardless of circumstances, perhaps more than most any other virtue.

● ● ●

PRAYER

Lord, You are my hope. Your goodness brings me out of darkness and keeps me from despair.

LOVE REQUIRES JUDGMENT

YEA, THOUGH I WALK THROUGH THE
VALLEY OF THE SHADOW OF DEATH, I WILL
FEAR NO EVIL; FOR YOU ARE WITH ME.
—PSALM 23:4

If you take someone you love to the doctor to be examined because of a suspicious-looking growth on his arm, you will want that doctor to bring judgment upon the growth and do whatever needs to be done to remove it. You won't pick a doctor who shows mercy to the growth or one who becomes fascinated with how it is its own living entity. Only judgment is acceptable.

I realize that sounds pretty silly at best to have a doctor who thinks like that, but I say it to make a point. There's no feeling of sympathy toward the tumor, nor is there any concern over what others might think. Judgment is the only acceptable response, as your love for that person requires such a reaction toward anything that threatens his well-being. Love requires that I fight for him by seeking for his protection.

We live in a world where we celebrate judgments all the time. But for some reason, if the judgment comes from God, it's considered cruel and unloving. My friend Mike Bickle made a statement on this subject that really helped bring clarification for me in this issue: "All of God's judgments are aimed at whatever interferes with love." Priceless. And so completely true.

• • •

PRAYER

Lord, help me to understand Your goodness at such a level that I see that You are good even when I'm walking through hardship. You are good. All the time.

LOVE STANDS FOR SOMETHING

THERE IS THEREFORE NOW NO CONDEMNATION
TO THOSE WHO ARE IN CHRIST JESUS,
WHO DO NOT WALK ACCORDING TO THE
FLESH, BUT ACCORDING TO THE SPIRIT.

—ROMANS 8:1

If I had a neighbor who showed aggression and violence toward children, I would do whatever I could to inform the authorities and protect the children. While I tend to lean toward mercy for people who are caught up in sin, I would refuse to do anything that would protect their sinfulness, which would continue to threaten the safety of others. Such carelessness toward "friends" is not love at all.

Love stands for something. It is honest and confrontational when necessary. It is not love to see someone you care for in a burning building and leave her there no matter how sincere she is, or how good of a person she is, or how rough her childhood was. Love requires action. Love requires judgment—"This building is on fire. Get out or you will die!" Love chooses the best. Love doesn't choose what simply feels good to us.

If God were hell-bent on bringing condemnation on all mankind, He could and would have accomplished that a long time ago by simply declaring the word needed to bring it about. The whole point of this book is that condemnation is not in His heart.

● ● ●

PRAYER

Lord, where I am filled with shame, please show me Your truth. Take Your light into the dark places of my heart.

JESUS BORE GOD'S JUDGMENT

FOR HE MADE HIM WHO KNEW NO SIN TO
BE SIN FOR US, THAT WE MIGHT BECOME
THE RIGHTEOUSNESS OF GOD IN HIM.
—2 CORINTHIANS 5:21

It is true that *"God takes no pleasure in the death of the wicked"* (Ezek. 18:23). Yet the fact remains, judgment has to happen because God is holy—He is perfect in beauty, with undefiled purity, completely separate from all that is dark and evil and totally driven by love in all actions, thoughts, and intentions.

Sin violates and contaminates all that He has made, creating a breach between Creator and creation. Yet judgment had to be released because He is love. Out of necessity He declared, *"The soul that sins shall die"* (Ezek. 18:20). That was something that came forth because He is love. Please notice that statement is in the same chapter as *"God takes no pleasure in the death of the wicked"* (Ezek. 18:23).

God cannot lie—it would be an impossible violation of His nature and being. But the most amazing thing happened. God chose to pour out the much-needed judgment upon His Son, Jesus, instead of us. Because of His great love for us, Jesus volunteered to take our place in bearing the penalty of death that each of us deserved. In doing so, He satisfied the appetite of the Law for our judgment.

* * *

PRAYER

Lord, You saved me when I could not save myself. Your great love for me has changed my life forever. You took my judgment.

ROCK THE BOAT

HIS NAME WILL BE CALLED WONDERFUL,
COUNSELOR, MIGHTY GOD, EVERLASTING
FATHER, PRINCE OF PEACE.
—ISAIAH 9:6

Love requires judgment if it's to be real love. Love without judgment is apathetic, lethargic, and passionless; it really isn't love at all. Any belief system that promotes conviction without emotional expression is more consistent with Buddhism than it is with the Gospel of Jesus Christ. It doesn't rock the boat. That is something that Jesus had no problem doing time and time again. Jesus was far from passive.

The position of "not rocking the boat" is often applauded as peaceful, when in reality it's a peace that can only exist where the person of peace controls the circumstances or setting. Jesus is the authentic Person of Peace (He is the Prince of Peace) who demonstrates what real peace looks like. He did this while being accused, persecuted, beaten, and crucified. Circumstances don't control, influence, or determine the reign of such peace, as it is superior in every possible way. It is anchored in a person who changes not.

Love is a person—God is love. He loves people to the point of sacrificing the life of His own Son on a cross. That zeal is beyond our ability to measure, and yet we're alive because of it.

● ● ●

PRAYER

Thank You for Your light. You have rescued me out of darkness and given me a fresh start. You have become my salvation.

ADJUSTING YOUR THOUGHTS TO MATCH SCRIPTURE

"IS NOT MY WORD LIKE A FIRE?" SAYS
THE LORD, "AND LIKE A HAMMER THAT
BREAKS THE ROCK IN PIECES?"
—JEREMIAH 23:29

Many who have started to catch a glimpse of God's goodness have followed their own logic and reason far outside of biblical parameters. That is always a danger. We all have convictions and ideas about what is true. I'm referring now to someone in the process of growing and developing in Christ, not the person given to a spirit of deception. As someone once said, we don't know what we don't know. But we must not try to make the Scriptures say what we believe; we must adjust what we believe according to the mandates given in Scripture. The Word of God cuts and prunes our original ideas into a truly biblical shape until they represent Jesus well.

We need the whole of Scripture to shape and enliven what we think and teach. Far too many try to change what the Scripture says to protect their definition or what they feel they've been learning. It is wiser to hold in tension two contradictory ideas than it is to twist what the Scripture has said, discounting the one that doesn't fit your ideal. Everything must yield to the Word of God.

● ● ●

PRAYER

Lord, give me eyes to see the secrets contained in Your Word. I want to know You well, fully convinced of Your heart.

THE TRUTH OF GOD'S WORD

SANCTIFY THEM BY YOUR TRUTH.
YOUR WORD IS TRUTH.

—JOHN 17:17

Who God is is revealed in what He says. He identifies Himself as the Word. In other words, He says nothing apart from who He is. His Word reveals His nature and manifests His presence. Jesus was never a broadcaster of truths He didn't live. Even the people of His day recognized this as a reason for His unequalled authority: *"Never has a man spoken the way this man speaks"* (John 7:46).

Many come dangerously close to criticizing Paul or Peter (or whoever has written the Scripture in question) and attributing what the writer said to his own biases. The thought is that Scripture contains teachings that are inconsistent with the teachings of Jesus. That approach scares me big time. That means the person who is critiquing what the Scripture writer has said actually has an opinion that has greater value and authority than what the Bible itself says.

It's so much easier to believe God, trust God, and ask the Holy Spirit to lead us into all truth. What I think, live, and teach must be consistent with the Bible, so I allow what is written to prune my definition until it will stand the test of God's Word itself.

● ● ●

PRAYER

Lord, I have purposed in my heart to believe You and trust You. Holy Spirit, please lead me into all truth.

WITH HIM THERE IS FORGIVENESS

FOR HE MADE HIM WHO KNEW NO SIN TO
BE SIN FOR US, THAT WE MIGHT BECOME
THE RIGHTEOUSNESS OF GOD IN HIM.
—2 CORINTHIANS 5:21

Forgiveness of sin is a primary focus of the New Testament message. This is a most incredible gift—we are forgiven. But part two of this gift is that our nature to sin is changed. The part that once again changes the landscape of life on planet Earth is that every person who is in Christ becomes the righteousness of Christ.

No wonder the psalmist stated this principle of forgiveness in the most profound way: *"But there is forgiveness with You, that You may be feared"* (Ps. 130:4). That has to be one of the most unnatural combinations of truths in the Bible. He forgives us, and because of that, we fear Him. As you can imagine, this kind of fear does not drive people from Him. Instead it draws people to Him.

He qualified us to receive the inheritance that only He deserved. I remind you that He alone is the One who lived without sin, blemish, or compromise of any kind. In all honesty, I would have been totally satisfied to have my appointment with hell cancelled. But for the Father to qualify me for the same reward as Jesus? That is as far beyond my grasp as any thought or idea could possibly be.

● ● ●

PRAYER

Father, I am amazed that You would qualify me to receive what You are giving Jesus. Your love for me is boundless.

FROM A PLACE OF TRUST

"HE IS THE ROCK, HIS WORK IS PERFECT;
FOR ALL HIS WAYS ARE JUSTICE, A GOD
OF TRUTH AND WITHOUT INJUSTICE;
RIGHTEOUS AND UPRIGHT IS HE."
—DEUTERONOMY 32:4

Some would say that because God loves people, and it isn't His desire to see the death of the wicked, people don't go to hell. That is a popular reasoning of the day we live in. It is true that hell was created for the devil and his demons, and not for people (see Matt. 25:41). But Jesus talks a lot about hell, outer darkness, weeping, and gnashing of teeth. It takes a lot of work to make the Bible say there is no hell for people and even more work to say everybody goes to Heaven.

This concept of Universalism is from hell itself, as it strips the Church of any sense of urgency and accountability for embracing the Great Commission. If Universalism were true, there would be little need for the bulk of Scripture, as it becomes pointless in a world where all roads lead to the same place. Once again, the Bible must be used to shape our thoughts and opinions, even when those Scriptures seem to defy logic and reason. It is from a place of trust we discover Him, the One who is superior in all logic and reason.

● ● ●

PRAYER

Lord, I want to trust You more, so I can discover You more. It is the desire of my heart to know You.

LOVING PEOPLE AT THEIR WORST

"A NEW COMMANDMENT I GIVE TO YOU, THAT
YOU LOVE ONE ANOTHER; AS I HAVE LOVED
YOU, THAT YOU ALSO LOVE ONE ANOTHER."
—JOHN 13:34

Standing with people in the midst of their problems seems to be a fading value. To stand with someone who is in sin is frowned upon, as it makes others think we support their sin. Jesus sure seemed to have a different approach and was called a friend of sinners as a result.

On a practical side, it serves no purpose to create an atmosphere that encourages people to freely exhibit their sinfulness without consequences. It's much wiser to stand with someone with issues if he wants to clean up his mess. Choices have consequences, good and bad. That is life. Our loyalty to one another must be solid, but it must not empower others toward wrongdoing.

As crazy as it sounds, unsanctified mercy has taken the place of true mercy. Unsanctified mercy empowers people toward sin without an awareness of consequences. True mercy is shown to people in trouble by loving them when they don't deserve it, but also by telling them the truth, working to bring them into a freedom that God intended for everyone. True freedom is not doing as we please. It's being enabled to do the right thing well.

● ● ●

PRAYER

Lord, teach me about Your mercy. I want to be merciful, as You have shown me mercy.

THE WORK OF CHRIST

"GO THEREFORE AND MAKE DISCIPLES
OF ALL THE NATIONS, BAPTIZING THEM
IN THE NAME OF THE FATHER AND OF
THE SON AND OF THE HOLY SPIRIT."
—MATTHEW 28:19

We've been living in the last days for two thousand years. The prophet Joel spoke of the outpouring of the Holy Spirit in Act 2 as that which would take place *"in the last days"* (Joel 2:28-29). So if those were the last days, we are certainly in the last of the last days.

Jesus had much to say about the days we live in: wars, rumors of wars, famines, earthquakes (see Matt. 24:6-7). It's important to note He wasn't giving us a promise. He was simply describing the conditions into which He was sending His last days' army with transformational influence.

Everyone's last days theology requires faith. For some it is a faith to endure until we're rescued. For others it's a faith to obtain in response to our commission. I'll take the latter. We are the most useless in our faith when our confidence for transformation depends on the return of Christ instead of the work of Christ. His return will be glorious! But His work set the stage for a transformed people to transform the nature of the world they live in. It is a glorious work, being done by a glorious bride that the Glorious One will return for.

● ● ●

PRAYER

Father, I want to carry out the assignment You have given me. It is truly glorious work! Thank You that, like Jesus, I get to reveal the Father.

HIS PROMISES REVEAL
HIS HEART

BY FAITH SARAH HERSELF ALSO RECEIVED
STRENGTH TO CONCEIVE SEED, AND SHE BORE A
CHILD WHEN SHE WAS PAST THE AGE, BECAUSE
SHE JUDGED HIM FAITHFUL WHO HAD PROMISED.
—HEBREWS 11:11

Many things recorded throughout Scripture go far beyond information. They are promises— something we are to believe God for. To keep the subject of promises in perspective, I remind you that Israel was given a promise of entering the Promised Land. Yet the generation that first heard that promise didn't enter it. Did God let them down? After all, it was God who gave them the promise. No. They had responsibilities in bringing about God's fulfilled promise. They became hard-hearted and tested God over and over again until God said no! to their entering His promise to them.

My friend Larry Randolph describes this issue best. He states, "While God will always fulfill His promises, He is not obligated to fulfill our potential." Some promises are given to us from God. They reveal His heart, His desire, and His purpose for us. But it's quite possible they may never happen. Why? Because they must be believed and acted upon before they become a reality for us. There is a role that we play in most of what God has declared over us. To blame God is simply irresponsible.

● ● ●

PRAYER

Father, I want to see Your will come about in my life. May my heart be extremely sensitive to Your leading.

CAPABLE OF SURVIVING THE BLESSING

"SEE, I HAVE SET THE LAND BEFORE YOU; GO IN AND POSSESS THE LAND WHICH THE LORD SWORE TO YOUR FATHERS—TO ABRAHAM, ISAAC, AND JACOB—TO GIVE TO THEM AND THEIR DESCENDANTS AFTER THEM."

—DEUTERONOMY 1:8

There are so many promises from God concerning the days that we live in, but many of us are blind to them. I think the main reason we become blind to these promises is that we are accustomed to being opposed, and we've definitely seen evil increase. That then becomes the standard by which we interpret what is coming our way. It isn't. We do not have an inferior gospel.

There is an unusual parallel with what the Church is experiencing and the story of Israel going into the Promised Land. It is sometimes frighteningly similar. It's as though God said, "The whole Promised Land belongs to you, but you'll inherit it little by little. If you get it too quickly, you won't be able to manage what you'll inherit, and it will turn around and bite you. Embrace the process, for in doing so I am making you capable of keeping what I give you, if you'll simply obey from the heart."

God gave us surpassingly great promises to help us navigate well during challenging days and circumstances. He is working to make us capable of surviving His blessings.

● ● ●

PRAYER

Father, Your wisdom astounds me. Even in the giving of Your blessings, You have shown me love and care.

DAY 86

BEHOLD THE GOODNESS OF GOD

AFTERWARD THE CHILDREN OF ISRAEL SHALL
RETURN AND SEEK THE LORD THEIR GOD AND
DAVID THEIR KING. THEY SHALL FEAR THE
LORD AND HIS GOODNESS IN THE LATTER DAYS.
—HOSEA 3:5

It just might be that the most overlooked evangelistic tool of the Church is the blessing of the Lord upon our lives. We've seen blessings abused, materialistic kingdoms built in His name, and other self-centered expressions. But when we react to the errors of others, we are prone to create yet another error.

The Bible says that others will see His goodness and will in turn fear the Lord. I wonder, how good does that goodness have to be for people to see it and actually tremble? It's hard to imagine His goodness in a casual or incidental manner bringing about that response. It would have to be so clear, and in my opinion so extreme, so as to be obviously manifested from God Himself, that people tremble with fear.

The promise is clear—God's goodness will be seen upon His people. Put on your seat belts! We're about to enter the journey of a lifetime. It's a time where opposition increases, the need for our help becomes more obvious, and the blessing of God separates us from others. Knowing how to steward such things is paramount to our fulfilling His heart to disciple nations.

● ● ●

PRAYER

Lord, teach me to steward well the blessings You pour out upon me and my family. May Your goodness and glory in my life be so obvious that people fear You and put their hope in You.

His Absolute Goodness

GOD BE MERCIFUL TO US AND BLESS US, AND
CAUSE HIS FACE TO SHINE UPON US. THAT YOUR
WAY MAY BE KNOWN ON EARTH, YOUR SALVATION
AMONG ALL NATIONS...GOD SHALL BLESS US, AND
ALL THE ENDS OF THE EARTH SHALL FEAR HIM.

—PSALM 67:1-2,7

The above passage contains two parts of Psalm 67. The first one says, *"Your salvation among the nations"* (Ps. 67:2). And the second one is, *"And all the ends of the earth shall fear Him"* (Ps. 67:7). What brought about the conversion of nations in this prophetic psalm? The conclusion is they feared God and experienced His salvation! But what caused them to see the heart of God and His nature to the point that they were convicted of their own sins and turned in repentance to Him? What caused such a miraculous turn of events?

Blessings. Blessings are what preceded both statements of nations coming to Christ—bless us so they know what You're like, and God shall bless us, and they'll come to Him (my paraphrase). No wonder the devil works so hard to undermine our confidence in His absolute goodness. It's that specific revelation that is key to a massive last days' revival, where there is a harvest of entire nations. The stakes have never been higher. Settling into the realm of His goodness has never been more necessary than it is now.

● ● ●

PRAYER

Father, You have given me the desire to reveal You to others. Bless me, so they will know what you are like!

THE CHALLENGE
OF BLESSINGS

"WHEN YOU HAVE EATEN AND ARE FULL, THEN
YOU SHALL BLESS THE LORD YOUR GOD FOR
THE GOOD LAND WHICH HE HAS GIVEN YOU."
—DEUTERONOMY 8:10

Blessings come with a challenge. No generation that
I'm aware of has been able to navigate a life full of
blessing while still serving God sacrificially. Blessings
create entitlement, superiority, independence, materialism,
greed, and so on. The problem isn't with the blessing of
God. It's us. I believe God would provide for us beyond
any of our wildest dreams.

While I don't want to make this term blessings about
money alone, it must include it. But what would that
blessing do to us? Many people only have a prayer life
because they have troubles. Who then would pray? Many
develop community because their personal needs are so
deep that they need others to make it through their week.

What happens when that need is not quite so obvious? Raising up a generation that can live with blessing while still bearing their cross is the challenge of the day. From my perspective, God disciplines us so that His blessings don't kill us. It's really true.

Because God loved Israel, He showed favor upon Solomon and made him king *"to do justice and righteousness"* (1 Kings 10:9). It basically comes down to this: favor upon me must benefit the people under my influence, or it is misused.

● ● ●

PRAYER

Father, I know You have great blessings for me. Help me to learn how to handle Your blessings well.

JESUS BROUGHT A FACE TO GOODNESS

OH, TASTE AND SEE THAT THE LORD IS GOOD;
BLESSED IS THE MAN WHO TRUSTS IN HIM!
—PSALM 34:8

Jesus came to reveal what we needed most: the Father. Tragically, that wonderful revelation suffers under the broken condition of our present family culture. Because so many have suffered under the abuse or neglect of their biological fathers, the wonder of this phenomenon is often lost.

On the other hand, there's never been a moment more ripe for this greatest answer to human brokenness and need. Most of the ills of humanity would be healed with that one revelation—Jesus came to set our focus, attention, and affection on the Father, who is good.

Our Father really is perfect goodness. That revelation is laced throughout the Old Testament with His continual display of mercy toward a rebellious people. Time and time again, Israel brought disaster upon themselves through worshiping idols made by hands and giving themselves over to the sexual sins of the surrounding nations. Yet when they cried out to Him, He delivered them without complaint or punishment. His goodness drips from page after page of Scripture. When Jesus came, He made it nearly impossible to forget the new standard, as He brought a face to that goodness. It became personified in Him. Goodness became measurable—taste worthy.

● ● ●

Prayer

You are the One who is a Father to the fatherless. You comfort those who mourn, and how You have comforted me!

Because He Is Good

For You, O Lord, will bless the
righteous; with favor You will
surround him as with a shield.
—Psalm 5:12

Blessings are manifestations of increased favor. Yet favor has a purpose. We are coming into increased times of favor and blessing, with greater and greater areas of responsibility. I'm not saying we're coming into a life of ease and self-exalting bounty. It's just that He is making it more and more obvious who carries His heart by releasing an increased favor upon them for influence. That is that mark of His blessing.

Our positions of increase are unto something. The problems that our cities and nations are facing have no answers outside of God. We, the people of unfailing hope, have the opportunity to serve and serve well, bringing the King and His Kingdom into the everyday lives of people all around us. He is putting something upon us that will help them to see Him. If I use that which God is placing into my charge for personal gain, I will find myself seriously disappointed. But if I can live with His favor and blessing and use it for its intended purpose, nations will turn to Christ. That is His promise. That is His Word. And it is so, because He is good.

● ● ●

PRAYER

Lord, please help me to use the favor You give me to benefit those under my influence. I want nations to turn to Christ as a fulfillment of Your word to me.

REFLECTIONS ON THE GOODNESS OF GOD

About Bill Johnson

Bill Johnson is a fifth-generation pastor with a rich heritage in the Holy Spirit. Bill and his wife, Beni, are the senior leaders of Bethel Church in Redding, California, and serve a growing number of churches that cross denominational lines, demonstrate power, and partner for revival. Bill's vision is for all believers to experience God's presence and operate in the miraculous—as expressed in his best-selling books *When Heaven Invades Earth* and *Hosting the Presence*. The Johnsons have three children and nine grandchildren.

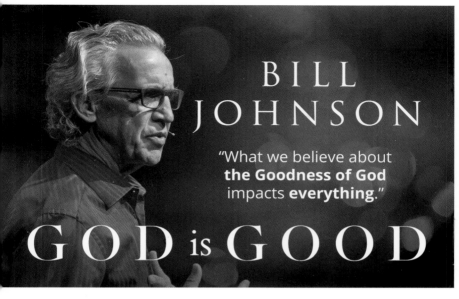
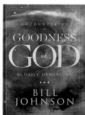
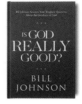
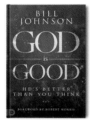

FREE E-BOOKS?
YES, PLEASE!

Get **FREE** and deeply-discounted **Christian books** for your **e-reader** delivered to your inbox **every week!**

IT'S SIMPLE!

VISIT lovetoreadclub.com

SUBSCRIBE by entering your email address

RECEIVE free and discounted e-book offers and inspiring articles delivered to your inbox every week!

Unsubscribe at any time.

SUBSCRIBE NOW!

LOVE TO READ CLUB

visit **LOVETOREADCLUB.COM** ▸